THERE WAS AN OLD WOMAN

There Was an Old Woman

Reflections on These
Strange, Surprising, Shining Years

Andrea Carlisle

Oregon State University Press   Corvallis

Cataloging-in-publication data is available from the Library of Congress.

∞ This paper meets the requirements of ANSI/NISO Z39.48-1992
(Permanence of Paper).

Oregon State University
OSU Press

Oregon State University Press
121 The Valley Library
Corvallis OR 97331-4501
541-737-3166 • fax 541-737-3170
www.osupress.oregonstate.edu

Oregon State University Press in Corvallis, Oregon, is located within the traditional homelands of the Mary's River or Ampinefu Band of Kalapuya. Following the Willamette Valley Treaty of 1855, Kalapuya people were forcibly removed to reservations in Western Oregon. Today, living descendants of these people are a part of the Confederated Tribes of Grand Ronde Community of Oregon (grandronde.org) and the Confederated Tribes of the Siletz Indians (ctsi.nsn.us).

For my sisters in age, whatever age that may be.

There was an old woman lived under a hill
And if she's not gone, she's living there still.
Baked apples she sold, and cranberry pies
And she's the old woman who never told lies.

—NURSERY RHYME, FIRST KNOWN PRINTING 1714

Contents

The Finding

A woman slowly opens a carved box.
She has come to the dark tower, she has found
the hidden room, and quieted the hound
that guards it; she has picked the rusty locks,
pushed open the reluctant door, and seen
the box among the shadows on its stand.
She lifts it. It weighs little in her hand.
She hesitates beside the fire-screen,
hearing the hound whimper, "Do not open it."
The woven peacocks in the curtain scream:
"To wake will break, to wake will break the dream!"
She draws her breath. She slowly lifts the lid.
Stones and darkness vanish. Nothing is there
but her, the grass, the silent, shining air.

—URSULA K. LE GUIN

PREFACE

A Wide View from a Far Shore

W hen you're old and you happen to speak the words "I'm
old" out loud, many people are quick to disagree. "You're
not old!" they insist, a signal of their feelings, known or buried,
that being old is not a good thing. To them, old is not a wide view
from a far shore but a dark sea you could get lost on due to some
failure of navigation. They try to rescue you by pulling you back
on course, a younger course, even if you don't want to go.

I've always liked old things—lockets with photos of forgotten people snug inside, scuffed books of essays by nineteenth
century writers, complete with inscriptions ("Dearest Eveline,
Congratulations on your matriculation. Love from Mother"),
letters written in ink on paper so thin you can see your fingers
through it, old dogs, mountains, rivers, oceans, prairies. If it's old,
lead me to it.

The chair in which I write this today is old, ivory-colored
wicker, with arms wide enough for solid human arms to rest on.
The arms that once rested here belonged to my friend Teresa's
beloved great-aunt, Marie Jordan Bell. Marie lived on a ranch

in Wyoming among animals dear to her. "My heart is with my horses," she used to say. She loved dogs, too, with a tenderness that might surprise people on either coast, given that ranch women are legendarily tough. Let us acknowledge Marie was that, too. At seventy-two, her pelvis was crushed when a horse fell on her, and she was told she'd never ride again. She rode again.

Why not say that when she sat in this chair on her porch at a hard day's end and looked out over the meadow and corrals, sipping her favorite bourbon, Marie was a living, breathing set of contradictions? This is what old women realize they always were and will always be. The lucky ones make peace with it, even though they can see this as something the world doesn't like to recognize. Old women are supposed to turn simple. And quiet. They're not supposed to own a fierce desire to live, let alone to ride again.

So let's say Marie, sitting in the chair day after day until her death at eighty-five, lived contentedly as a bundle of contradictions. She might have longed to feel the tide of youth rushing through her veins while, at the same time, she was becoming increasingly curious about how the years were changing her. She might have liked thinking about how wonderful it would be to take her fastest horse for a gallop across miles of green pasture again and yet felt immense satisfaction in sitting as quiet and still as a blade of grass. Probably long before she suffered a heart attack in her eighties, she would have come to appreciate the human heart itself as a curiosity—so handy as a metaphor in youth for speaking of love but also a real muscle with a real job in a human being, to keep blood coursing.

Some people make this discovery only when the heart muscle forgets its job and does other things—makes up a new rhythm for the bones to dance to or drops the task of pumping blood absolutely everywhere throughout the entire body, as if that's a kind of ridiculous goal, or gives out a great sigh now and then. *Whoops! Didn't mean to scare you*, says the heart, which is still trying to do its best, just as the young romantic tried to do her best to learn how to keep love going.

It feels good to reach an age when you can truly understand the heart's complexities. It's a little cathedral within from which hard-won lessons, eternal mysteries, love, and sustenance flow, a constant author of replenishment. Sometimes people learn all this early on, but many of us can only come to deeply know the heart if we get to live a long life.

Marie, the ghost who sits in this chair with me, may have wandered now and again over to the gravestone in the tall grass where a favorite dog of her younger life, Mike, was buried. She may have sat by Mike's grave for a while wishing she could feel him at her heels again as she worked through each chore of her day, just as I long for my own youth sometimes and as I wish that I could whistle my dogs back to my side and jog with them again along the Oregon coast.

We miss those we love who are no longer with us, not to mention capacities we once had and cannot have again, but missing is no reason to deny what we have now. No one could be more surprised than I am to find herself at this stage of life, yet here I am, as many millions of us are. Turn away if you don't want to listen to what we have to say, but don't try to talk us out of our place here on the shore. You'll arrive, too, soon enough. We're all headed in the same direction, after all, and so it's only natural to name the place we are looking from and to comment on what we can see from here.

PART ONE

Old Is a Long Walk

Old is a Long Walk

On any given day, a visitor to the houseboat moorage where I live might see a group of two to six older women trooping to the upriver end of the walkway together where they will pause to move one of four white stones that sit atop a wooden railing. I wonder what she would think. Some sort of crone ritual?

Stone in place, the women will turn on their heels and head toward the downriver end, turn again, revisit the railing, move a second white stone, and so on. Four loops back and forth, four stones moved equals two miles, the goal. Although the white stones are not sacred but practical, they were carefully selected from the gravel in the parking lot.

If it's cold outside, the walk is brisk; if hot, it's more leisurely. Whatever season, the visitor would notice that the walkers are always talking, often laughing. Occasionally, one of them might stop the others and point up at the sky or down at the river so she can announce the sighting of something interesting. If it's in the water, she speaks in a whisper so as not to scare it off.

Longtime river dwellers, these women only stop for notable things. They may tilt their heads back momentarily to gaze skyward for the flight of a blue heron that's screeching like the rusty hinge of a country gate opening wide, but they're not likely to slow down. The herons regularly fish at either end of the walkway. They're part of the community. A muskrat scurrying into the brush along the riverbank as their footsteps approach barely gets a glance. Over the years, they've observed generations of sleek cormorants sitting on tall pilings, wings spread wide to dry damp feathers. They don't take these things for granted, but they wouldn't halt mid-stride to look at them.

That said, although there's nothing new about otters on this part of the river, the women still like to watch them. They might stop to observe a family of them at play on the riverbank, and sometimes one or two of the pups might come swimming closer to satisfy their own curiosity. The women will stop for a row of western painted turtles sitting on a log tied to one of the houseboats, too, or the sighting of the lone sea lion, head the size of a basketball, who arrives in winter from the Pacific to gorge on upstream fish, or a bald eagle sailing into the shadowy upper tier of the cottonwoods lining the riverbank. An osprey circling over the river on its hunt will also get their attention, as will a beaver swimming close to the walkway, leafy branch in mouth, carrying on as if it doesn't see them because, *Oh well, it's just the old human females*, nothing to slap your tail against the water about. One or two of the women might talk to the beaver as they would to any other neighbor, and the beaver will more than likely always assume they're talking about constructing an underwater home and respond with a guttural "Huh-uh," which is taken to mean, *Go find your own building stuff.*

If she has been patient enough to linger and observe (perhaps at the top of the ramp, giving her a good vantage point), the visitor might mention the women when she descends the slanted eighty-foot platform and arrives at whichever houseboat she's visiting. "Yes, I know who you mean," the owner will say. "They're out there almost every day."

Walking improves health in all sorts of ways, say the doctors: blood pressure and blood sugar levels lower, weight is maintained, mood lifted. But the idea of moving, even only for a short distance, can sometimes feel like a big challenge to old bones. It makes it easier to do it together.

When both of us were in our fifties, Lou, in her eighties now, started walking with me and my dog, Boon, a foxhound/greyhound mix who needed lots of exercise daily. We tagged behind him on a loop trail over on the island across from the houseboats. If we went late in the afternoon, Boon's bright white fur coat acted as a beacon ahead of us when twilight fell before we got all the way back to the trailhead.

After Boon died and time became more of a crunch thanks to changes in my job, we switched to the walkway, a flat, quarter-mile-long cement structure, like a sidewalk but on flotation. It runs in a gentle curve from one end of the moorage to the other. Sometimes it moves with boat wakes but never enough to throw anybody off balance.

Julia, in her sixties, started walking with us about five years ago, and now we are often joined by Joan, also in her eighties, and occasionally by two more sixty-somethings, Carol and Melissa. All of us work (social worker, teacher, artist, writer, animator, filmmaker), and all of us take charge of the maintenance of our houseboats and life within them. This can involve hauling wood or other fuel, including groceries, down the ramp, and carrying our recycling and garbage up the ramp.

Except for Julia, we have all lived on this channel of the Willamette River for decades. I came in the 1970s and can't imagine living anywhere else. Lou preceded me by a year. The others came later and feel the same. Although she's been here the shortest amount of time, Julia has now joined us in knowing the moods of both the river and the Pacific Northwest weather. If the day offers even the tiniest bit of fitness for walking, we call or text each other with time suggestions, then pull ourselves away from our computers or other tasks and emerge from our portals at the appointed hour, sniffing at the fresh air like Mole of *Wind in the Willows* who'd been cooped up working on his spring cleaning until he cast his work aside with an "O blow!" and scooted himself up and out into the day.

Some articles about fitness suggest using a smartphone app or a graph to chart daily activity. Only Joan is faithful to her app and will stop periodically to tap, tap, tap at her watch. She won't quit walking until she reaches her daily goal of ten thousand steps. The rest of us give our allegiance only to the small white stones.

Online sites dispensing advice often demand more than some of us at a so-called "certain age" may be willing to do. *Lift weights. Take a spinning class. Make your heart pump.* This assumes that everybody wants to live longer. If we're healthy in all or most ways and financially okay, finding ways to extend life can seem like a good idea, but not all older people will see more and more years in a positive light. For those experiencing relentless poverty, debilitating health conditions, severe depression, dementia, extreme loneliness, or chronic pain, for example, longevity may not be a goal. When we get to be older, we realize that things can happen to any one of us that would make the idea of living a lot longer undesirable. Longevity for the sake of longevity is like money for the sake of money, or a long marriage to the wrong person so that you can boast about the number of years spent together.

In our cases, we want to make healthy choices, for the most part, and walking is one of them. I think what helps maintain at least the mental health and general optimism of our group is not only the walking but the community of walkers. We are women who like being together even though, in all other ways, we're independent. Some swim or kayak or canoe on their own. As for me, I take solitary walks, too. They clear my head and give me time to reflect in a way that a community walk often does not.

Sometimes I stroll the walkway by myself with a camera to see what I can catch of the river's life; later, I might add the images to my Instagram collection or post for friends on Facebook. I like social media for connecting with old friends as well as writers, artists, and photographers I haven't met but whose work I admire. (I've never read so many good novels and contemporary poetry in my life as I've found on Facebook, thanks to poets and writers so often recommending the work of others; it's a feast.) Although some of the photographs I take may end up on social media, I'm not thinking of these networks when I take a walk alone. My focus is more on the network within myself: connecting the dots, tying up loose ends, questioning, appreciating.

Because my mother lived to the age of one hundred and was in my care for the last seven years of her life, I'm more aware than many that old age can go on for quite a long time, up to forty years in fact, with some living even beyond one hundred. Four decades is not what people usually think of when they think "old age," but it's a fact for more and more of us. That's twenty-eight years longer than childhood, if we consider that childhood ends at twelve; thirty-three years longer than adolescence; and equal to the years between twenty and sixty.

When I'm out alone on the walkway or wandering down familiar trails in the nearby woods or climbing the steep hill to the main road and back down again, it's not unusual for my mind to fasten on specific questions; there may still be plenty of life left to answer them, if not the same deep wells of energy that I've known in the past. I ask: *What am I focusing too little of my energy on these days? Too much? Who among my friends have I not reached out to in a while? Which battles before me are worth my fight? Why are some thoughts about certain people or subjects recurring? What is this repetition trying to get me to notice or let go of?*

I solve problems on these walks, or try to, and make plans, but lone walks are never all about thinking. My pace is slower than when I'm walking with other people. I pay attention to the seasons in a way that doesn't involve judgment about the weather but an attempt to experience it, trying to *know* the sensation of an icy wind on my face or the way sweat collects on my brow on a hot day. I can feel the gentle, feather-light rain that falls on my bare hands, hear the splash of my boots in the puddles as I cross the parking lot and head for the path into the woods, where I fill my lungs with the cleanest air for miles.

The Japanese call entering the forest to rest and cleanse the mind *shinrin-yoku*, which translates to "forest bath." The trees I've walked among for over forty years—alder, Douglas-fir, aspen, cottonwoods, maple, and red cedar, to name a few—have aged along with me. Whenever I walk the trail along the riverbank and come across a heavy bough that has been ripped from a trunk and fallen from a great height during recent high winds or an ice storm, I'm sad for the break. I don't go so far as to hug the tree, but I might inwardly nod to it. The life force in this forest is strong. A lost limb here and there won't diminish it.

The path along the riverbank ends much sooner than it used to when I arrived here in the late 1970s. It narrows, and overgrowth now comes between me and the even older trees I know are ahead, but I don't mind letting them have their privacy. Even a short walk among the mossy trunks nearer to home always helps me return to myself.

Although I know old age can last a long time, I'm also aware that you never know where or when your own path through it could be foreshortened. This is true at any time of life, of course, but the awareness, when it shows up, is keener. One day when I emerged from the forest path, some questions came to mind unbidden, as though the forest had been whispering them into my ear while I was walking, and when I reached the open space above the moorage, I could hear them. The piercing whistle of the eagle pair that had caused me to glance upward and wonder which tree they'd choose this year for their nest; will I hear it again? The train's horn that comes blasting in over the trees from the tracks not far down the road, is this the last time for that sound to disturb my quiet? I leaned over to take in the exquisite fragrance of daphne at the top of the ramp. *How many times have I done this?* I wondered. How many times will I do it again? How many more figs from the little tree on the riverbank or blackberries straight from the fence and into my mouth in how many more Julys? Or the refreshment of cool air rising from the river as I walk down the ramp on a hot day? How many more goslings will I see lined up in a fluffy golden thread between their mother in the lead and their watchful father in the rearmost? Or the reddening of the sumac along the riverbank? Jewelweed and water iris rising from the logs on the breakwater in spring, my cat Riley curled up under the strawberry tree on the edge of the float in front of my houseboat—how many more times?

I reminded myself to pay attention. Those high-pitched chirps of the blackbirds in the bushes: Listen. That web construction going on between two clumps of maidenhair ferns: Look. The wave from my neighbor, Tim, eighty-three, seated on the bench next to the red tulips is an invitation to join him and chat for a few minutes: Sit. Given our years and the fact that many of us have stepped out of the hubbub of daily living as if out of a steady wind, we have time now to gather ourselves together, check in on who we are, where we are, what we bring, what's brought to us free of charge just by living through a day.

Is it morbid to think about things coming to a close, maybe sooner rather than later? I don't think so. It feels realistic. No need to dwell on it, but given that I'm now in my seventies, I'm thankful that I recognize the facts. It feels like a home base from which I marvel at the good fortune to have been here at all, let alone for the whole span of a human life.

My neighbors and I go outside for exercise because we want to be outside. We wouldn't live here if *outside* wasn't an essential component of who we are. A houseboat moorage is all about the outdoors. Canoes and kayaks cover floating decks built for their storage and for sitting and watching birds or for stepping onto paddle boards, or climbing into a boat, or diving into the river to swim.

Not all of us do all of these things, but outside calls, no matter. As a child in the Midwest, I lived in the open air as much as I could. If I did not now find myself outside for part of the day for the sake of breathing fresh air, then something about the way I'm living my life would be false.

My mother, on the other hand, didn't want to go out for most of her adult life. She became anxious when the wind blew through her carefully combed hair and protected it with her hands. She didn't enjoy being hot to the point of sweating on her clothes. While my father dug in the garden, my mother stayed inside and kept busy with chores, happy to see him when he brought in produce and fat pink peonies to arrange in a vase.

For years I thought my mother must have been an indoor-only human all her life, but when she moved nearby in her very old age, she told me stories about her childhood—the way she ran bare-foot through the dirt streets of her small Dakota town and out into the countryside with her five sisters and little brother, all of them climbing, jumping, running, skipping, exploring the prairie with noses, eyes, ears, and feet. I knew then that those years of staying inside as a grown woman had been the opposite of her true nature, that she'd been sold a bill of goods, along with millions of other women of her generation and my own who'd been told to value personal beauty and tidiness more than sun on skin, breeze on face, heart uplifted by the sky's expanse, legs stretched out in response to the deepest inner voice we have as physical beings, the one that whispers *move, move, move,* if only because moving feels good.

Other girls and women may have had a different experience altogether, but the message my mother and I both received in small towns in the Midwest was to ignore that inner voice. For example, at her high school and at both of the high schools I attended, there were no physical education classes for girls after the eighth grade. The voice of our midwestern culture came across loud and clear. Nothing needed spelling out. Considering the models offered and the values expressed, it didn't take much for us to understand our place. Stay inside and move the body only through the motions of the daily grind of domestic work for as many decades as are possible for you.

There have always been some women who refused to listen to the prevailing orders and chose the experiences they wanted. My friend Patricia ran her forty-first marathon at seventy-one. Carolyn, in her seventies, was an Olympic athlete as a teenager and has stayed active throughout her life. She walked the Camino twice in the past decade and will walk it again.

Younger women mountain bike, hike up trails to camp by themselves in the wilderness, swim miles of laps at the community pool, row on crew teams, skydive, and participate in all sorts of other outdoor activities. More and more women of the older generations are joining this wave of the physically active. Yet, I know women in my age group who say that movement at even the most basic levels still feels daunting.

Surprising things can happen to anybody, though. When she came to Portland, my mother took herself outside quite often. The trees and flowers, many of them different from the ones she grew up around, drew her out. She did squats daily, too, trying to make sure she'd be strong enough to continue walking on her own. Her goal was one hundred a day and she usually met it, even into her late nineties. In her recliner, she did leg lifts, also one hundred a day. Before she got out of bed, she performed a series of movements that got her blood going. *Who is this woman,* I asked myself, amazed at how change can happen in even the oldest among us. Always strong, she now became determinedly active in a way I never would have expected. She showed me that we can bring new things to being old.

Sometimes it takes a village even to make a small change like a daily walk. Some of us at the moorage might not walk as much or even at all, if it weren't for the fact that we can do it together. It's not always fun to walk in pouring rain; even harder to go out in summer heat, but if we set out after dinner, we can manage it. Now and again, in summer, we'll walk up the ramp to visit the community garden, a giant spiral of flowering plants and a side row of raised beds for vegetables. In July and August, we might follow that visit with a walk over to the small Buddha statue that sits near the blackberry bushes and pick berries in the dying light of day. We linger until we've filled a large yogurt container or two with dark, plump fruit. Of course we could pick berries alone, and each of us has done it alone many times, but there's more pleasure in picking together.

If we decide to stay on the walkway in summer, we move at a slow pace between the thick heat of dusk and the Hour of the Bats. At around eight-thirty the bats start to swarm between the houseboats and cruise along the river, gobbling up mosquitoes. Sometimes they zip up to the dock lights, hoping to catch a mouthful of moth or binge on the dozens of gnats caught in the spider webs hanging there. We feel grateful to the bats for clearing out the mosquitoes, but they are many and fast and everywhere.

In fall and winter, when darkness comes early, we often walk along the walkway even in moderately heavy Pacific Northwest rain. Many times we've walked when it was snowing and ascended the ramp to admire the shawls of snow covering the forested hills across the road. We circle around and across the wide patch of land used as the moorage parking lot.

As soon as spring yawns itself into longer days, the land at the top of the ramp beckons again. We take one another to the pear tree, the fig tree, the first unfurling of purple iris and orange tulips, the weighty white camellia and scarlet rhododendron blossoms, and the daffodils and roses planted on the long skirt of grass along the river side of the parking lot.

Our almost daily walks on the moorage are not meant to be aerobic necessarily, although sometimes they are. When one of us texts, suggesting a time to meet on the walkway or up on land, she is simply putting bodies in motion. These walks take us out into the fresh air as well as into one another's lives. We discuss events in the neighborhood, the health status of various neighbors who have fallen ill, minor and major personal troubles, the height of the river, the coming or receding weather, art, books, movies, politics.

All the while, we might each be pushing our own stones uphill. So be it. Together, it can be a more pleasant push. Although we know that most of our lives are behind us, not ahead, this won't stop us from sliding the white stones over to a new spot, one at a time, until we reach our goal.

Each time along our way, we stop to pet Chesca, the old tortoise-shell cat, at one end of the moorage, and Jiggs, the fourteen-year-old Lhasa–Shih Tzu who likes to lie in the middle of the walkway near the upriver ramp. Sometimes we catch a glimpse of my cat, Riley, who watches us pass by from her perch in the laundry room window, each time registering those few seconds of the parade with surprise and interest. *There they are! Wait! Where'd they go?*

"Old is a long walk," I would answer her (and the curious visitor, too). We will continue on for as long as we are able.

The Second Coming of Age

I spotted the old-fashioned desk pressed against a neighbor's basement wall. At thirteen I was nimble enough to leap over a mountain of laundry and wriggle past teetering floor lamps, rickety tables, bedsprings, and other castoffs not quite ready to be tossed away but no longer useful to the family that lived upstairs. When my fingers pulled on either side of the desk's front panel, brass hinges released and a writing surface dropped forward, revealing cubbies for ink bottles, pens, envelopes, and stamps. I'd never before seen anything like it and fell in love. Mrs. Coburn, who managed a large batch of children and a cluttered house, had dispatched me to her basement to find it and take it home. I couldn't know how important it was to become, how it would save me during those years of my first coming-of-age, but now I wonder if maybe she knew.

Black hair pulled back and bunched into a messy cluster, always looking as if she'd dressed in a rush—forgetting at least one button and completely ignoring belt loops—Mrs. Coburn was the opposite of my pretty, well-put-together mother. She didn't appear to be the sort of person who would have time to consider the best interests of a new kid in the neighborhood. She was a continually sought-after anchor for her own many offspring, which included Mary, twelve, my new friend in the household. In the rare moments none of the children needed her, she preferred sinking onto the worn floral sofa with a book to housekeeping. This made her an anomaly in a small midwestern town with the unofficial motto, *Cleanliness is next to Godliness.* Two other things distinguished Mrs. Coburn from other mothers: a juice glass of red wine always sat near wherever she happened to be, and one hand always held a cigarette, except when she washed dishes. Then, the cigarette hung from her mouth and the smoke streamed upward, assaulting eyes that squinted to protect themselves. Ashes long as caterpillars dropped occasionally into the suds.

I washed the dishes at my house, but none of the Coburn children helped their mother with this chore, even though they came in a range of ages, from around five all the way up to the oldest boy soon to join the Navy. If Mary and I happened to be doing homework in the Coburn kitchen, sometimes I'd look up and see her mother's hands working away in the soapy water while her smoke-filled eyes gazed out the kitchen window, seemingly at something other than the strip of front lawn and her husband's paint company truck in the driveway. I did the same thing three doors down at the sink in our kitchen. A narrow backyard with tall trees on either side offered a pleasing view from the window, but when I stared at it, the yard wasn't what I saw while my hands worked in the hot water. I saw nothing. I felt nowhere.

I remembered Mrs. Coburn and the desk the day I started poking around in *The Coming of Age,* by Simone de Beauvoir, published in English in 1972. The book jacket's inside flap records a note Beauvoir sent to her publisher when asked about the purpose and character of the book she wanted to write: "Are the old really human beings? Judging by the way society treats them, the question is open to doubt."

In the exhaustive discussion that follows, reaching far back into history and investigating a range of other countries and cultures, Beauvoir brings forth the physical, emotional, psychological, and practical aspects of longevity. At the very least, she wanted to raise questions and urge people to look at this time of life honestly, with perspective, not with stereotypes and ignorance.

I fell into a few random chapters that, here and there, reminded me how challenges I'd faced in adolescence mirror those I'm meeting up with again now. I'd thought about and written about that period quite a lot because of the tragic death of my oldest brother when I was thirteen. But as I read Beauvoir's ideas and remembered how easily the young are dismissed by almost everyone, I considered the enormous adjustments required by those years, even without tragedy. The question Beauvoir raised to her publisher could apply also to people going through adolescence: Are the young really fully human?

In both our first coming of age and our second, we can see that getting very lost is a real danger, but, then again, a lot of interesting, rewarding, and even exciting new realities arise, too. During both periods nature forces us into a different physical self. A hormone storm announces the start of each of these transformations. Our bodies experience changes, some of them alarming, that we cannot stop.

As if that isn't disruptive enough, feeling alone sometimes rides sidecar with biology, at least it did for me when the estrogen faucets turned on at one age and off at another. At thirteen, I had friends but not the language for what it felt like to lose my brother, and this lack cut me off from the others. Now, I feel able to talk about things but spend a lot more time by myself. A sense of aloneness can exist for many of us, despite the fact that a multitude of similar bodies were then and are now going through big changes. In junior high and high school, young people are physically together and can openly joke or commiserate with one another, if they want. But older people don't come together in a common arena, such as a school, every day. We stand apart while set apart.

As adolescence moved along, I noticed that adults—teachers, parents, even strangers—would sometimes strike up a peculiar conversation around me. They spoke about a future in a way that went beyond the often-repeated question of childhood, "What do you want to be when you grow up?" They looked at my changing body and seemed to feel free to talk about anything from whether or not I had a boyfriend (meaning did anyone love me?) to future marriage possibilities, or lack of them, to whether or not anyone should invest in my education, to speculation about the possibility of getting booted out of the house when I reached eighteen. Nobody inquired too deeply into my thoughts about any of this, but they did agree a "someday" existed out there for me and it would be filled with the usual, expected things for white girls from small midwestern towns.

In these later years, there's also talk about what lies ahead, but it takes on a worrisome tone and there's rarely a mention of investment or options. Simone de Beauvoir asserts that an older person is not perceived as important to the future and just barely as someone having a future. At one point she writes, as maybe only a French philosopher would, that an older human being is "no more than a corpse under suspended sentence." I was taken aback, but I knew what she meant. Not many are looking to invest in an older person, except maybe herself, if she's able.

People don't see old age as an extension of adulthood, which it is. To some extent, at least, the perception makes sense because of ways the body transforms. The changes can seem to put a body into the camp of different or *other*. Young and middle adulthood bring changes too, but we have more control there, and we face fewer restrictions or threats of restriction, with less chance of not being taken seriously. Nobody asks, "Are adults really human?" Except when seen through the prejudices of people who are racist or sexist, adults are human.

But then when you reach fifty or sixty, you may find yourself in the margins where nobody expects much more from you, and whether or not you're fully human falls into question once again. Lying as they do along adulthood's margins, nothing very important goes on anyway, says society, in either youth or old age. Adolescents are not quite yet members of the Useful Furniture Division, which gets to live upstairs with everything happening in the rushing richness of life; many of the old are shuttled off to the basement bearing scars and considered used up.

The marginalization of both young and old was the first similarity that struck me as I continued on with *The Coming of Age*. It's common to think that usefulness comes only with absolute freedom; no freedom, no use. Yet, at both times of life, I've noticed that I've expected to be treated as a free and equal person. I've expected myself to contribute and to have others find my contributions worthy. Unfortunately, my expectations weren't met as a teenager, and it doesn't happen a lot of the time now. At both times of my life, I've felt a subtle but firm emphasis by others on not *who* but on *what* I am: I'm a child/I'm an old woman. *Am I really a human being?*

My oldest brother, Bruce, had died by suicide, which was the reason we moved from the house where it happened to a different one across town. Bruce had been someone I loved, looked up to, respected, and now missed; losing him made my first coming of age a dark time. Fraught. Our household shrank in a few months from six to four: my parents, my sister, and me. After Bruce's death, my traumatized, miserably unhappy brother Michael had begun acting out in ways that upset my parents. They had been advised—by a psychiatrist, of all people—to send him away to join the Navy, even though he hadn't finished high school. My parents approved the recommendation and off he went into a life-time of unresolved feelings, alcohol, and unhappiness.

Sadness and loneliness were the daily forecast for the rest of us in our new home a few doors down from the Coburns. Despite this, like many other adolescents, I experimented with talking back to my mother, testing boundaries, pulling away from dependence on others so that I could explore life on my own. I longed for any freedom I could snatch up. Like my peers, I wrestled with needing safety as I felt drawn to independence, but moments of independence relied on permissions doled out by others.

Likewise, during this second coming of age, I'm experiencing a time in which grief comes with the territory—the loss of parents, relatives, friends—and autonomy is greatly treasured. Again, threats to independence have to do with permissions allowed or refused by others. A catastrophic fall, a severe illness, a loss of income, memory, sight, or mind, and those others can revoke my freedom, in pieces or all at once. I pushed for full freedom as a young person, and although authority pushed back, occasionally being free and being dependent overlapped. I might have become old enough to drive a car at one point, for example, but not to drive it at night, a restriction that found an echo in my sixties, until I had cataract surgery.

Once, others saw a girl developing into a woman; now, when others look at me, they see a woman of a certain age or even beyond whatever they think "a certain age" means, and they have whatever assumptions that come with that—probably not anything about development. From my own point of view, the girl in the mirror at thirteen bore little resemblance to the one who headed off for college at seventeen; the face in the mirror at age sixty looked more like the me I was used to than the one I see now, more than a decade later.

In *The Coming of Age*, Beauvoir takes into account not only the physical but other disorienting realities, those that occur out of sight for both the old and the young: the boredom lying in wait thanks to exclusion from the mainstream of life and economic anxiety for the same reason. Interestingly, the proximity of our childhoods is also something we have in common. Every adolescent is aware she's emerging from childhood; older people often like to tell stories about themselves as children. The fact of a childhood, in both cases, is amazing: *I* was a child.

And then there's time. Simone de Beauvoir observes the strange way different ages experience time itself, something my friends and I puzzle over: *Why does a day, a week, a month, a year, a decade go by so quickly now?* In childhood, it's almost as if time doesn't exist; we're not yet adjusted to any sort of framework for it. For a good chunk of my childhood, I couldn't even "tell" time, but time, for that matter, had nothing much to tell me. I stayed focused on everything I encountered because it was all new; days seemed long as I leisurely unpacked each minute. Now, my experience is that not much happens to either me or the world that has never happened before. Because there's not a lot that's new enough to lose myself in the novelty of it, time feels like a thoroughbred racing to the finish line, a streak of life—some color, some blurring, hoof beats striking the earth faster and faster.

Travel, Beauvoir explains, allows for a reappearance of newness. An unconscious grasp of this notion may be why so many people dream of traveling when they retire. Even if a clock will still be ticktocking away, it'll be a hometown clock, unrelated to the traveler's concerns. She'll be away, in a place where life itself acts in a timeless way.

For all its insights, *The Coming of Age* is not an optimistic book. Disaster looms in nearly every aspect of growing older. To Simone de Beauvoir, things turning out well now and then may not have seemed like a plausible theme to include in a book on the subject of longevity and its consequences. But whenever she discussed the parallels between adolescence and late life, it gave me a chance to fall into wondering about them. This is probably why the desk bobbed up into consciousness, and when it did I got excited by the idea that there might be yet another way our later years can mirror adolescence.

I thought about coming-of-age stories and the way a reader is drawn into how a young protagonist (someone not so different from *her*, the reader must understand) steps into a challenge un-prepared. She struggles with obstacles and comes out the other side, changed forever and ready to experience life as a more com-plete person. In other words, readers (or viewers) come to know and identify with a character who faces intimidating change but still has a future.

It should go without saying that this can also be true for the sec-ond coming of age, but it's not assumed to be part of the story of growing older. It's rarely even mentioned, let alone written about. Even so, it happens. It's happening right now, in fact, in many places, with many millions of older people.

When I read coming-of-age stories as a young person, I noticed the main character always made it to the other side, even if it seemed many times that she would not. Because I identified with that character, I found comfort in the chance I could make it too, even when all the roadblocks and sadness and confusion seemed insurmountable. This gave me a kind of faith.

At some point in these stories there is often a gift of some kind given to the protagonist. In any variation of The Hero's Journey, a template based on mythology and written about extensively by Joseph Campbell and others, this gift can be an actual physical thing, like a special weapon, or something more abstract, such as an opportunity. It doesn't matter what it is as long as the main character receives something that will move the process of transformation forward.

I won't go into all the particulars of the hero's journey structure, which includes not only ordeals and gifts, but reversals, returns, and more. Joseph Campbell's work is interesting, as is the work of many who write about this subject, but they're looking at the skeleton of a story. Meanwhile, authors have known for a long time how to put meat on those bones and are at home with what they're doing when it comes to transformation and working magic.

Betty Smith provided a library as the gateway to a better life for Francie in *A Tree Grows in Brooklyn*. In *I Know Why the Caged Bird Sings*, Maya has stopped speaking because of trauma, but she retrieves her voice when Bertha Flowers leads her into poetry. Aunt Raylene is someone the abused girl, Bone, in *Bastard Out of Carolina* can finally trust. Jeannette, whose natural sexuality keeps getting quashed by a mother in thrall to the family religion, gets help from Miss Jewsbury in *Oranges Are Not the Only Fruit*.

A critical piece of a positive outcome has to do with how main characters respond to what shows up for them. They have to do their part too, which is to draw on their own resources to make use of what's offered in order to further their own growth. As a young reader, it took me a while to figure out this key feature. The circle won't complete itself. When I read *Jane Eyre* for the first time, for example—maybe even the second or third time—I didn't see this element of the story, but eventually I came to understand that a chance to work as a governess in a grand house, and better yet, to be loved for who she is, may seem like a gift for the impoverished Jane; even so, the position and the love offered are not enough for her to live the life she wants. When things in that house become complicated (it's called Thornfield for a reason), she leaves and spends a year in a place where she starts again from nothing, even giving herself a new name, and there she gains the strength and balance to deal with her conflicts about her future. Building this more balanced self allows her to open herself to the changes she wants, not those others want for her. This inner growth is how she earns the privilege of having a better life.

This piece about meeting the opportunity is the part that's easy to forget, but I think remembering it is so important to the time of life I'm in now. A gift—even if it comes in the form of an incredibly wise person, even if it's a *wizard*—won't be sufficient if I want to create any sort of future for myself other than the proverbial downhill. If something helpful comes along and I'm awake enough to catch on that it could be important, I need to meet it with something in myself in order to close the circle. This is the only thing that will make it potent enough to take me somewhere. I don't happen to believe this is some "method" that belongs to storytelling but a truth of life also found in stories, and most obviously in stories about coming of age.

Although Beauvoir makes comparisons between young and old, she's clearly more interested in writing about the old. She only compares the two groups now and then. Mostly she wants to tell her readers the ways in which older people are treated and where and why. There's no talk of coming-of-age novels, at least not in the long sections I read. Nothing about gifts and this critical fact of needing to meet them—if any come along—with something in oneself. No reminders that it might be a good idea to look back at our adolescent selves so we can learn from an earlier time in our lives when we faced similar psychic, emotional, social, and physical hurdles.

Even though Beauvoir didn't speak directly to these things, there was no reason that I or anyone else couldn't draw our own connections and ask ourselves how we managed the drastic change from childhood to being an adult. What was it we told ourselves about ourselves? How did we survive it and maybe occasionally even thrive? Because we were capable of meeting the challenges of a large cluster of changes before, we can probably do it again. I find strength in knowing this about myself. And what about the gift? Was there one, more than one? How did we meet it? Is there something now that's offering itself for use? It seems to me there's a lot of potential at these two thresholds, adolescence and old age, but we have to be able to see it and reach into ourselves in order to release it.

When I first reflected on this, I saw how my young self had once been bedeviled by all sorts of obstacles, diminishments, restrictions, and rejections while my body and psyche altered in ways out of my control. Even when I began to look like someone I didn't recognize as myself and society started to treat me differently because of that, I found ways to accept reality and move forward. It occurred to me that finding my way through adolescence was even harder than finding my way through some of these same sorts of things now because at least now I know who I am. We didn't know ourselves so thoroughly then, and it's likely we didn't have language for whatever parts of ourselves we did know. Even so, we nevertheless crossed storm-whipped waters; at least most of us did.

My brother sadly did not complete the journey, and his death by suicide added PTSD to my particular passage through adolescence. I can't say for sure how much of my staring out at our backyard over a steaming sink and feeling nothing and nowhere was the state of mind for a "normal" adolescent exhausted by the pressure of all the changes, or PTSD, or a combination. I'm not sure anyone can be certain about how these things play out inside of us, even though we want to tidily wrap them up, but I know now I wasn't alone. Based on the words of many other women and men I've read and spoken to over the years, it's apparent that huge numbers of us traveled the whole hormonal/social/psychological course of those years while facing other burdens: abuse of all kinds, racism, bullying, neglect, psychological harm, poverty, lack of education or access to clean air, food, and water. When I reflect on the ways I managed the challenges I faced, and when I learn about others who faced much more daunting odds and found their way, it boosts my confidence in terms of facing what lies ahead for so many of us now.

Looking back, I could also easily spot the most important gift I received during that time. I couldn't believe my luck when I carried the little desk into my new bedroom that day in late summer. Finally, something I'd chosen myself lived in the room my well-meaning mother had fixed up for me. My previous bedroom had not been fancy: a dresser, a lamp, white sheets covered by a plaid spread. But in this new house, the bedspread was a hazy field of pastel yellow and pink flowers on a white background. She'd painted the walls a sunny yellow and hung gauzy curtains with lace trim on the windows.

I knew my mother would have loved to see anything other than the flannel shirts and short-sleeved cotton blouses with pearled snaps like the ones on cowboy shirts in a small closet opened by pulling two sparkling glass knobs. When she showed me a photo in a catalog of a girl my age wearing a pair of black velvet slacks with a white ruffle-collared blouse and patent leather shoes, I was horrified. It felt jarring even to wonder if I might one day soon want to wear something like that. The equivalent now would be someone handing me a catalog of urns and asking me if I'd like to order one for my cremains. Thanks for thinking of me but *not ready*.

The shelves in the twin cupboard on the other side of the window seat contained my rock collection in a laundry detergent box, some dead bugs slowly disintegrating in jars, and a few feathers, pussy willow twigs, chestnuts, and colorful leaves picked up from sidewalks and vacant lots on various outings around town while out on my bike. All came from shelves in my former bedroom.

Even before the new bedroom and its trappings, I'd known something was up. Two puffy nubbins, disturbingly pinkish brown at their centers, swelled painfully on my chest. My arms and legs shot away from my torso, their awkward lengths causing them to unexpectedly bump and tangle with each other. I dreaded more change but also felt curious about it. The unknown pressed in like a dark forest—scary, but also fragrant and deep with possibility. Something within it called me without words, a faint chorus of exotic birds. I couldn't stop myself from walking in their direction. I loved my rocks and dead bugs, but I could feel those new songs working their way into me. Every day I both yearned to know what the forest held and swore I'd keep away from its terrors for as long as I could.

By the time Mrs. Coburn's desk entered my environment of flowery bedding and a box of rocks, I was a mess of worry. The more I caught on to the magnitude of the changes headed my way, the more I lived in a constant mind spin of what to do, how to be. Neither the bedding nor the rocks offered any option other than either to fight hard to stay a child or choose how to be a woman from an unappealing menu of offerings. The desk came when I needed a safe place to put myself in the midst of all that change. But how had Mrs. Coburn known this?

On hot, muggy nights that summer, I'd spent a lot of time on the flat roof of the Coburn house, right above the master bedroom. Mary Coburn and some of her many sisters and brothers held slumber parties there and invited neighborhood kids. A long string of us would file up the stairs to the second floor, climb a short ladder nailed to the wall of the master bedroom closet, heave ourselves up the last, steep ladder step and through a narrow hatch, then toss our blankets and pillows around the tarred surface open to the sky and settle in.

Mr. and Mrs. Coburn, in their bed directly below, left the closet light on and the rooftop hatch propped open so that if anyone wanted to wander back downstairs, they'd be able to find the ladder.

We squirmed for a while on itchy blankets, swatted at mosquitoes, told jokes, and giggled. I don't remember exactly how the last act of every one of these evenings began. I was neither the oldest nor the youngest one there, but once we grew quiet it fell to me to tell a story and tell it loud enough for the whole crowd spread around the rooftop to hear.

I'd always told stories to my parents and various relatives, but now, on the Coburns' roof, I'd found a new audience. They listened to me make up characters and push them into one tricky situation after another, until at last everyone fell asleep under the night sky. Then I closed my eyes.

When I revisited this memory, it occurred to me that maybe Mrs. Coburn overheard all or parts of those stories. Had she thought I could use a desk of my own where I could write them down? For whatever reason she offered me the desk, I thank her for hours of a special sort of freedom all my own in a troubled time, a freedom unconnected in any way to usefulness or being all right or not being all right, being a girl or being a woman. It freed me even from grieving the loss of one brother and the prolonged absence of the other. As soon as it took its position along the wall opposite my bed at the end of that summer, I sat down in front of the secretary, opened the panel, picked up my pencil and a tablet, and escaped for the first time into writing my stories down. I concentrated. I brought myself to the task with all the imagination I could muster. Together, the desk and I closed a circle whose necessary existence I'd never even known about until then.

While the act of writing swept me away in one sense, in another it gave me something to hold onto. The desk served as a little boat when I felt lost, and it carried me to characters and places. In its company, I would always come to a story that seemed to be waiting for me to see it. Finished pieces passed around in study hall gave me a way to connect with my classmates.

I continued to write as adolescence stretched on, taking it more seriously in college and beyond, but it wasn't until my early sixties, when my mother moved to Oregon, that writing once again fulfilled all the things it had fulfilled when I started out. In keeping a blog about her and our time together, I found myself writing more than I had for decades. I felt the companionship of other daughter caretakers who followed the blog, and it surprised and pleased me that so many, including people who didn't have a parent to take care of, wanted to follow Alice's news, history, friendships, romantic escapades, even her sorrows. She and I still disagreed on clothes, but we found so much more to share than earlier in our lives.

So it was that my mother herself along with the habit of writing that began long ago became the gift at the entrance to my own old age. My practice of writing about her was as much of a bulwark against the pressures and uneasiness then as the desk and story writing had been for me at thirteen when faced with that often overwhelming time of life. When I wrote pieces about our being together, I escaped from anxiety about financial pressures and new limitations on my freedom because of caregiving, as well as fear about becoming old myself. Also, she set a good example. The blog gave me the opportunity to confide the realities of longevity to others in a realistic but palatable way.

Now, in my seventies and without her, I'm keenly aware of aging every day. The difference reminds me of how I felt when turning thirteen versus turning sixteen. This time, I know that eventually the forest will turn dark and deep. Period. Since there was no choice allowed in the matter of entering it, sometimes I feel trapped in an echo of my adolescent dread. Yet here, well beyond the early years of its mystery, most of the time I'm finding it quite a lot less scary than I thought it would be. On the other side of it, I won't find a career or possible children or any other possibilities once seen as rewards for the suffering of teenage years. Yet now, as during those early years, I'm finding satisfaction along the way and a lot of it is still sourced by writing, doing it when I want and for whom I want, as I did then.

Some time after reflecting on all of this, I asked my friend Judy if she found herself returning to things she'd done during her own coming of age years. She responded that she had "a keen memory of hearing a song lyric when an adolescent and then feeling a strong need to create the elements of it three dimensionally." "It's Only a Paper Moon" became a diorama in a shoebox: the moon passing over a cardboard sea. She added that no one in her family encouraged this song in a shoebox idea, but she did it anyway. Then Judy spoke of a cancer diagnosis that occurred at the beginning of her sixties. "I returned to this (idea) after my cancer diagnosis and treatment and felt a great relief after I made a small diorama of myself in a birch bark canoe sailing into the sky among the stars."

Now eighty-two, Judy makes both dioramas and books. One of her books, in the shape of a red accordion, folds open exactly as the instrument does. With paintings and text, the book tells the story of a young girl beginning to play music for the first time on her new red accordion, as Judy once did.

My friend Diane, who has not attended church since her youth, told me she has started playing old hymns on the piano for the melodies and harmonies. They remind her of the pleasure of singing in the church choir when she was in her teens. Other friends mentioned spending as much time as possible outside, playing the guitar, running, even smoking pot again—all things they'd loved when girls. This makes me wonder how many women in their later years are picking up these threads and pulling them into their current lives.

My family left that little Minnesota town and moved on to a slightly larger one in South Dakota. I never saw Mrs. Coburn or Mary or any member of that family again, but the desk rescued from the topsy-turvy basement of the Coburn house stayed with my parents for a long time after I left home and one day found its way back to me again. It sits near my bed and contains photographs, letters, cards, and a few journals. I write at my kitchen table. From here I can watch herons, geese, osprey, eagles, and cormorants fly past my houseboat window. In these years, they are among the gifts offered, and I meet them with appreciation and gratitude. Sometimes it's as simple as that to close the circle. I learned how to do it a long time ago.

Poultice

During the first year of the pandemic, I felt as shut away as Miss Havisham. I decided it was a good time to try to clear out some of the cobwebs of my past. I'd start with my home office and get rid of all kinds of things. It didn't take long to see that the difference between Miss Havisham and me was that all she'd need to do about her past was shove an old wedding cake and dress into a garbage bag. My task involved thousands of pieces of paper in the form of old letters, journals, notebooks filled with my writing, cabinets filled with students' writing, and albums and boxes of photographs. But there was nothing else to do, so I started in.

About a month into the project, I came across a box of photographs from my mother's side of the family. The first black-and-white picture I picked up was of my Aunt LaRue. It showed a striking young woman with dark hair, an easy smile. She wore a simple white dress and looked happy, maybe even a little bit sexy. On the back my mother had written: "She saved my baby."

I remembered the story, though not the event. I was only six weeks old when LaRue had saved my life. Outside the Bismarck boardinghouse that my grandparents ran, the winter temperature regularly dropped into single digits at night and rose no higher than the teens during the day. I'd been born during a blizzard in late November, but the January sky was free of snow the day my mother and grandmother, after listening to my nonstop coughing and difficult breathing for many days, began to be afraid that my lungs would soon give out altogether.

Everybody in the cramped household had been poor long before the Depression had started and were even poorer coming out of it. Doctors were expensive and rarely called on, even for babies wracked by coughs. Had my father been there, he might have left things to the womenfolk or he might have called a doctor. After all, his mother had once been married to one, and among her friends she counted doctors' wives. My father, though, had no say. He was in Germany fighting in the war. My grandmother decided my trouble must be pneumonia and sent for the second oldest of her six daughters, LaRue, the family healer.

LaRue is an old name. It means "one who dwells near the path." My aunt lived with her husband and young son quite a way off the path, in a small house on the Missouri river. She arrived at the boardinghouse with an onion from her pantry, a piece of flannel, and some hope. She sliced and sautéed the onion, let it cool slightly, wrapped it in the flannel and placed it on my chest. No one knew how or where LaRue got such ideas, but they often worked out. Sure enough, with the poultice in place, tiny bronchial tubes popped open and expanded in my infant chest.

About fifty years later, Alice happened to remember that day and told me about it. She attributed my restored health entirely to her sister. "LaRue can come and touch your forehead and turn your pillow over and you start to feel better," she said at the end of her tale, as if this explained my aunt's knowledge of onion poultices and pneumonia, and maybe it did. In any case, I thanked

LaRue the next time I traveled back to the Midwest for a visit.

"Oh, you're welcome," she said matter-of-factly in her deep, murmuring voice that seemed to have absorbed the ways of the Missouri. She made it sound like being summoned to that boardinghouse with the expectation that she could save a baby's life had hardly inconvenienced her at all.

Sometimes the layers of a family story peel away through the years with each telling or memory of it, until one day the impact hits, something you haven't been ready to look at squarely before. I placed the photo back in the box that night and headed to bed feeling almost startled to be alive seventy-five years after my life had depended on a young woman and an onion.

The task of cleaning out the office didn't go as quickly as I'd hoped. I had to keep stopping so that wave after wave of feeling could flow through. No safe harbor where I could shelter offered itself. Whenever I looked at their photographs, love for my grandmother, my mother, and her five sisters overwhelmed me. I missed them all, but I felt relieved they weren't locked away inside the assisted living centers and nursing homes almost all of them had ended up in. They would have been so lonely during the pandemic because each had been accustomed to going out, seeing people, and receiving visitors. Gone now, every one. Alice, the last of them, had died five years ago.

What's difficult when you start opening drawers and filing cabinets you've avoided for many years is that you remember what it felt like to have a whole life before you. In your thirties, forties, maybe even fifties, you might come across something and think, *Oh, here's that hilarious letter from Mrs. Luce, our neighbor in Wisconsin, who died decades ago. I'll keep it and read it again someday.*

One particular filing cabinet was my *someday* mother lode. With its cache of ancient letters, cards and postcards, maps, itineraries, cassette tapes, journals started and abandoned, address and date-books, its sheer bulk reflected the dementia we live with almost all our lives: we actually forget we're going to die. Thanks to the pandemic, though, the possibility of imminent death was unavoidable. So when I found a small black sketchbook in this cluttered cabinet, you'd think I'd have thrown it in the Goodwill bag. Had I ever used it? I doubted it. Was it likely I'd use it now? No. I'm a word person, a keyboard person. Yet I hesitated.

I remembered the sketchbook had been given to me almost five decades ago by a supportive partner who must have noticed me doodling while talking on the phone, the only time I ever did anything like that. When I opened it, I found two pen and ink drawings: one of Michael, the giver of the sketchbook, and one of me. Meant more as caricatures than attempts to show us as we were, they struck me as quirky and funny. I flipped through the rest of the pages to see if I'd drawn anything else and found nothing. I knew the reason was lack of confidence. The only other time I'd ever tried to draw was at age ten or so, and then my obsession, like so many girls at that age, had been horses. If your parents can't buy you a pony, draw one. No horses lived nearby, so I made them up. I worked hard but felt disappointed in the results of my efforts and decided drawing was beyond me.

Had it come to mind to look at a book about horses or even to try to imitate a cover of a book about a horse? *Black Beauty* was probably on my bedside table at the time. But no, that hadn't occurred to me. If it had, things might have been different, but "copying" from a book—copying words anyway—had been drilled into me as forbidden. My ten-year-old brain may have concluded all copying was bad. I had no artists in my family and no art teacher in the rural Minnesota town where we lived at the time to tell me otherwise. I believed pictures should come from me, and I couldn't make them come. Holding that sketchbook I'd forgotten existed, I realized I hadn't seriously tried to draw anything other than those two caricatures for sixty-five years.

At that point in the pandemic, I was long past hoping that things would return to life as usual any time soon. High stress had become the norm. Daily news about the virus swirled around us like a blinding snowstorm, dropping cold statistics and even colder promises of more misery to come. Most of us wore masks when we went out. Some news programs shared the faces of a few of those already lost, often older people who, only days before, had been out and about with friends or petitioning for necessary changes in some law or repairing something or on a run through the park with their dog—that is, completely alive. Some of the many who were dying now in nursing homes had been otherwise in good health, recovering from a broken hip or a faulty knee and planning to return home after a few weeks of rehab; instead, their lives closed in strange beds in strange rooms, without family or friends. Assisted living facilities also became petri dishes for the virus. Protection against getting sick seemed to depend almost entirely on politics, news sources, and levels of risk aversion.

Despite the fact that not all people beyond fifty or sixty have a health condition, *old age and underlying conditions* walked hand and hand in the media, including social media. Soon this conjoining spurred cries among an alarming number of young people, who thought sacrificing old-and-going-to-die-anyway people was okay if it meant returning to normal. What with their primary *underlying condition* being old age, how could a few months or years more on earth matter to them?

When they responded at all, older people cried out that they didn't *want* to walk off into oblivion for the convenience of everybody else. What about that daily run in the park with the dog, the time they wanted to spend with family and friends, their research, the books they were writing, the care they gave to someone who needed them, the animals that needed their attention and love, the law and medicine and teaching and preaching they practiced, the wounded birds they knew how to mend, town councils they served on, online classes they organized or attended? What about reading, watching movies, taking photographs, traveling to see friends or children and grandchildren, cooking, sex, and the thousands of other reasons people, regardless of age, prefer life over death? Yet, day by day, the pandemic revealed more of the foul core of ageism.

What would returning to normal look like anyway, I wondered as I sorted through my relics, aware that there was no *return* to anything but actual physical places in this world, and sometimes not even those? If the two oldest generations disappeared (and took everything they knew with them), what exactly would be *normal* about that? I couldn't think of a time any younger person had known life without old people, so how exactly did *normal* get associated with this hope? If I missed my own old people every day— my parents, my grandmother, my aunts and uncles—how would these young people feel later, pandemic over and their own elders gone, those same people, they might suddenly remember, who so often knew precisely how to love and listen to them?

I watched the COVID-inspired hashtag "boomerremover" boil to the surface. Despite having experience with disabilities among family and friends and despite reading and writing about ageism, this surprised me. I realized I'd actually had no idea just how deep the hostility ran toward the older and most vulnerable in our society.

With no access to sit down dinners with my friends, no social life that included the occasional event or movie or any sort of entertainment other than what my various screens could provide, with my thoughts about my writing or even what I might make for dinner constantly disrupted, my composure started slipping. All the lives lost and the sickness endured by those who didn't know if they'd live or die from the virus kept me awake at night. I needed something to help me get through each day without dwelling on loss and fear of loss. I needed room to breathe without focusing on all that was wrong and could not, in any way—at least not at that time—be corrected.

And so, even though it seemed unlikely I'd ever open it again, I continued to hold onto the sketchbook. Given eye problems that include double vision and a maddening, blurrying number of floaters, a rational voice tried to nudge me toward reality. Wouldn't it be a waste of time to try to draw? Wasn't I too old anyway to start something like that? And what about the fact I had no idea what I'd even want to draw, let alone any idea how to do it? Why add frustration to stress and sadness?

A countering voice, quieter but also reasonable, urged me to carry the empty book into the living room and place it on the coffee table and see what happened. No harm in that, said this voice; it reminded me that at least the cataracts had been removed a couple of years ago. I could see much better now. And anyway didn't I love the feel of this object, smaller and lighter than a paperback, its black cover smooth, all those pages empty, waiting, and hadn't it been a gift from someone who is still in my life, still my friend, and whom I still dearly love?

I shut off the light in my office and closed the door behind me, sketchbook in hand.

The sketchbook didn't sit on the coffee table untouched for long. One morning I turned off the news and rummaged around at the back of the back of a kitchen drawer until my fingers gripped a stubby #2 pencil I felt certain I'd once spotted there, probably the only pencil in my house because I prefer pens. I fetched the sketchbook and opened my laptop.

Reading and writing had always been my escapes from both emotional and physical pain, but now I couldn't concentrate on either one. I figured even ten or fifteen minutes of scribbling shapes on a page might calm me down long enough to lose track of and come back to a center I hoped was still there. Maybe people put helpful videos on YouTube for those of us who had no idea how to draw. I'd find them.

The first random how-to-draw video I found was all about noses. I couldn't think of a reason not to watch it. The voice of the woman telling me how to make a nose happen on a piece of paper (I saw only her hand at work) came across as pleasant, direct, and, unintimidating. She didn't know a thing about the awkward horse sketches from my childhood or my floaters or double vision or the fact that I'd never had a drawing lesson and had been fortifying a lack of confidence in this area for over six decades until it was now as thick as Hadrian's wall. News that the sketchbook with its pristine pages had resided in a filing cabinet since 1975 had not reached her. Without ever meeting me, she wholeheartedly believed I could draw a nose.

I drew noses. Lots of them. When arriving at the end of my ability to improve each drawing, I leaned back to take in my finished result. Each time, even though it seemed impossible, I realized that I'd actually drawn something that looked more or less nose-like. I felt astonished, and not garden variety astonished but jaw-dropping. How could I have done that?

I watched the video again, this time paying more attention to how my teacher worked with ovals, circles, and shading. I listened more carefully as she alluded to many things that she seemed to sense would never have occurred to me regarding a human nose: how it exists in lines, curves, angles, shadow, and light; how it relates to the cheeks; how it folds at the edges like wings and builds in light and dark all the way up to the eyebrows.

I may have been an old woman alone in my house with my head on the line during a pandemic while millions of people tweeted their hopes that I and my peers would all die so they could get back to work and parties and cafes again, but in my life noses reigned. Even when not actually drawing them, they jumped out at me from magazines, postcards, book covers, and calendars. They populated my daily landscape like wildflowers, all different from one another, each one posing a new challenge to the No. 2 pencil. A newscaster might become her nostrils, tip, or bridge and not the spokesperson for the end of the world as we'd known it. An actor might become the ball of his nose and the creases running alongside its wings and not a man playing a love-starved widower denying himself a happier life. Who knew the flat spot at the top of a nose was called the root, and from this root the nose rises into its channels and bridge, lifting itself from the backdrop of a face and reaching out like the stigma of a flower, taking in smells as the stigma takes in pollen?

I might have gotten carried away thinking about it, but I couldn't blame myself. It had never occurred to me that a nose consisted of parts with names like root, wings, and folds. Until now, I'd either admired a nose, if I noticed one at all, or I'd ignored them, and that was the end of it. Although I wasn't seeing many people in real life and those I saw wore masks, drawing brought the facts of a human face closer and demanded that I look.

I remembered the awe my mother felt, at the age of ninety-nine, when I started bringing children's picture books to her apartment because her eyes had failed to the point where she could no longer read text. One of these books was about the development of a human embryo. I watched as she slowly turned page after page, following the journey from embryo to fetus to—many pages later—a newborn baby. Alice had given birth to four children but had never taken a sex education class; not only the fact of conception through birth, but she, her own body, seemed a marvel to her. My own exuberance at the accomplishments in the sketchbook—my enthusiasm around discovering the wonders of the body at my late stage in life—made me feel closer to my mother.

Given the dire straits of the planet, was it wise to be so enrolled in escapism? I wondered about this from time to time as I dabbled away at drawing. Shouldn't I try to face reality and be serious, even though I couldn't change anything that was happening? Then I'd remember that I couldn't finish reading a book and I was regularly having nightmares. Even if I ignored the news, by early afternoon I always felt exhausted. But I felt lucky to be on my own, free to avoid others if I wanted and as much as I wanted. After years of living alone, isolation probably felt less painful to me than it did to so many others. Besides, I had neighbors I walked with regularly, and friends who called and even visited outdoors at a safe distance occasionally. I was extremely lucky and knew it.

I couldn't *not* face reality most of the time anyway. I sent money to politicians who might change things. I signed petitions and wrote letters urging people to vote in the upcoming election. For those sick or dying or feeling lonely and as hungry for touch as I, there were candles to light. One night before I fell asleep, I decided to try to telepathically send comforting thoughts to strangers in hospital beds who felt scared and cut off from those they loved. It wasn't that I particularly believed this helped. What evidence existed that it did? But I did it anyway, and it became a habit. I'd imagine their faces. Or I'd hear of someone whose face I did know who was now sick with COVID. I'd try to send the known people and the unknown others love. I tried to stay with them, drawing breath in, breathing out with an audible sigh. During long nights when I woke sweating from a nightmare, I used meditation to lay healing thoughts on their congested, painful chests, like a poultice carrying the spirit of Aunt LaRue.

Nobody could escape the relentless menace of the pandemic, especially nobody old, but I understood anyone who wanted to get out of the way of the threat for even a short amount of time, and I saw it happening. Quilts, jigsaws, embroidery, bonsai, calligraphy, hand-knit sweaters and socks, crocheted scarves, and other creative works filled social media posts. So many animals found new homes that some shelters emptied out. Release from the pressure for even a little bit of time, however it happened, felt mandatory. Maybe I couldn't save my hair from turning thin and falling out, each strand barely hanging onto a puny follicle. Maybe I couldn't help my sleep, once a peaceful escape of its own and now splitting open at random times with wide-eyed worry about the coronavirus on one hand and fascism on the other. Maybe I couldn't avoid waiting impatiently for daylight. But when daybreak finally came, I could grab the sketchbook and let another drawing video lead me on. My stubby pencil got so short my fingers couldn't hold it, and then one day a box of Blackwing Palomino Pearls from my friend Justin came in the mail. I bought a sharpener to keep their velvet leads pointy and sharp.

Thanks to my online teacher I soon began drawing mouths all over the pages of the sketchbook, dozens of mouths in different shapes and sizes. I liked their minute, barely visible lines, their dark corners. Lips obsessed me. And that odd dip in the flesh above the middle of the upper lip, what was that for, evolutionarily speaking? How come I'd never noticed it much? Did chimpanzees have it? I checked. Vertical lines, yes, but no dip. I found the feature in humans hard to draw convincingly, but I liked trying, and I liked thinking about it as I imagined reasons it might have ended up on the human face. Thousands of years of puckering up for kisses? Millennia of humans whistling their way through forests in the dark to keep fear at bay? Sipping from ancient rivers with reeds used like straws? Or maybe *Homo sapiens* noses were sensitive to a fresh planet engulfed in pollen and plants and prone to running, running, running night and day until a wee valley formed and stayed? I didn't want an answer. I only wanted to move the pencil and bring down the eraser to ruffle the page when I'd made a mess of it.

The act of sketching became my pandemic poultice. It drew out the toxicity of the present frightening moment and let me inhale the whole of whatever I chose to look at instead. It tamped fear down while I focused on learning to see familiar things in a new way. Peace came when I felt a willingness to try. Pathways in my brain opened that had been stuffed up for decades by thoughts of *I can't* or *I don't do that* or *I've got no talent for it.* I breathed in satisfaction when I got an intended result or anything close to it.

Drawing gave me sensual pleasure, amazement, delight, faith that the world and I remained connected, no matter the fragmentation the news people reported. I encouraged myself to keep on, even though no artist would be likely to call my drawings good or even fair. Judgment, even well-intended critical comments, weren't of any interest to me. I loved the feel of my seventy-five-year-old hand moving with purpose and daring to fill a blank space, loved the fact that my seventy-five-year-old brain kept up with the teacher's instructions, delivered in a calm, pre-virus, nothing-at-stake sort of way. She became the art teacher I'd never had, and eventually I did a little research and learned she lived in North Dakota. I celebrated the synchronicity of finding the photograph of LaRue, finding the old sketchbook, and finding her all around the same time, a healing triumvirate. The teacher was the living voice, the wise one, she who dwelled by the path and pointed the way.

With drawing, unlike writing, I could be mobile. My unhappy back thanked me when I walked around outside, pencil and sketchbook in hand. I could stand in front of a tree and draw the bark and moss. One day I heard a woodpecker in the forest above the houseboats and scanned the trees until I found it. Although it's one of the few birds who will stay in one place for more than a minute, my pencil proved too slow to catch it. Still, I liked trying.

It didn't matter if a drawing of a woodpecker, a fallen limb, or an old boat slowly deteriorating on a trailer at the back of the moorage parking lot didn't quite come together. I could always try again or turn the page and start something else. Sometimes I brought my camera to capture rabbits and squirrels, zooming in as close as I could get and later drawing their images in detail. In summer and fall, the community garden offered plenty of subjects: flowers and vegetables, a bench, a wooden, slat-backed chair, the nearby stone Buddha sitting with his back to the woods and facing out into an open field.

When drawing, my mood turned serious and playful at the same time. I only wanted to try to make what I saw on a piece of paper, not judge myself or try to get better at it. Only the making mattered. And what, after all, did *getting better* at something mean, anyway? Drawing itself, without care, was better than any bettering could be, an engagement free of ambition. It moved into my heart the way love does, for its own sake. We may have been walking through the valley of the shadow of death, but my pencil and my sketchbook comforted me, day after day.

Now, whenever I move the pencil across the page and make shapes and shadows, my breath calms, my mind quiets. I still think of drawing as a form of LaRue's poultice. Each breath draws in peace and each exhale releases whatever fear or tension the present moment might hold, keeping passageways and possibilities open.

My aunt who made the poultice that saved my life may be gone, but I echo her in a few ways. My middle name is LaRue, first of all, and like her, I live with a river outside my door. Also, I keep an onion and a piece of flannel on hand these days. Earth is a dangerous place to be old right now, and I hope to remain here a while longer.

Living in the Family Museum

W hat shall I do with the scarred dresser that crossed the sea in steerage with my great-grandparents in 1880? Josephine, a pregnant and impoverished girl from Oslo, made the journey with her arms crossed tightly above her belly; her husband, Christian, mentally fragile and increasingly dependent on alcohol, kept one ice-blue eye on his expectant wife and the other on his stoic parents, who had just said goodbye to Gudbrandsdalen, the valley where their ancestors had farmed for centuries.

The dresser landed first in a worker's cabin at a sawmill in Wisconsin where Josephine and her mother-in-law worked as cooks, Christian and his father stacked lumber onto wagons, and Christian drank up most of the money he earned. After a few years of service there, it joined the family for a jog west by train; it made the journey in a cattle car, a parakeet in a cage on top, a cat and newborn kittens snuggled in one of its drawers, and a cow roped to it. After arriving in North Dakota, the dresser sat within a sod hut on a homestead that yielded little. (Josephine squirreled away the butter and egg money behind a block of dirt wall so Christian wouldn't steal it to buy alcohol; she wanted to leave something to her three daughters.)

There on the prairie, far from the green hills of Gudbrandsdalen, the two old folks, my great-great grandparents, died. A couple of decades later, Christian and Josephine, who did not grow so old, died as well. The reliable bureau then occupied the corner of a bedroom in a rented house in a pioneer prairie town of three hundred souls and contained some of the hand-made clothing of my grandparents and their seven children. By the time I met this stalwart family friend, my grandmother was a widow in her sixties and used it to hold her flannel nightgowns, handkerchiefs, wool mittens, head scarves, brush and comb, and other sundries. I never dreamed it would one day be mine and that I would have to fret about its destiny.

In an article about older people and downsizing, I read that my children, if I'd had any, would reject what is now called the "brown furniture" of the past, furniture like this dresser. They'd prefer the stackable, the modular, the easily moved. Would they be interested to know that at the age of four I stretched up high as I could to deposit a squirming baby rattlesnake into a Kleenex box on this dresser's top because I was being called to lunch and needed to stash my new playmate somewhere for the time being? Would they like to know that the baby snake was never seen again? I'd disown these nonexistent children if they didn't care to hear that story.

But what can we who are past fifty, sixty, and beyond expect of those who follow us? Can we ask them to hang onto something that once held meaning for a family but has served its purpose? A valuable heirloom is one thing, but should far-down-the-line descendants be asked to take on, for example, a heavy and heavily used bureau that once resided in a rustic farmhouse in southern Norway?

No one explicitly asked me to take this dresser; it was understood by my Aunt Mattie, its caretaker after my grandmother's death, that someone would take it and the likely someone was me. I drove to Bismarck with my friend Teresa to fetch it after Mattie died. We actually wrapped it in protective plastic, as if a bump on the road could injure it more than a bouncy trip across the plains on a train while acting as anchor to a cow and home to a litter of kittens, serving as a receptacle for humble clothing in a dirt-floored sod house, and surviving seven children dipping into and out of it. Safe in its plastic cocoon, we snugged it into Teresa's van with a few other odds and ends from Mattie's life.

Sometimes I regret that fetching. For almost twenty years the bark-brown dresser has been sitting in my bedroom in Oregon, mismatching the light, modern lines of my home with its blunt, stocky shape, present as a faithful dog who will never die or leave me, one I cannot put up for adoption to anyone because a) I don't have the heart to kick it out after 150 (or more) years of family service, and b) no one else would want it. It's a peasant piece, made of wood roughly gouged from a primeval Norwegian forest by someone without a measuring stick. It stands thirty-eight and a half inches high and forty-three and a third inches wide, with four broad drawers. Its maker must have predicted valuable possessions for it to hold because each drawer has a large keyhole worthy of a pirate's chest (key long lost).

This history of lockability seems to have seeped into the bureau's sense of importance because the drawers put up a struggle whenever I try to open them. You'd think they were fighting to protect a store of jewels and not my socks and piles of well-worn sweaters. Yet, those stubborn drawers are the single charming thing about it. Their pulls are carved right out of the wood itself and are in the shape of fat, round fruit with trailing leaves. Grapes? Lingonberries? Marionberries? It's a reflection of my conflicted relationship with this dresser that I have never tried to figure out exactly what sort of fruit they are supposed to be.

I probably wouldn't be so conflicted if this were my single piece of ancient, valueless, scarred-up family furniture to daily observe, protect, and worry over as if I were a guard at the Getty, but that's not the case. I took a few other pieces from Mattie's house—a coffee table, for example, that looks like it's been a theater prop for several hundred plays, and her little scratched cherry wood desk, as well as letters, diaries, photographs, and newspaper clippings about the comings, goings, and significant life events of people long dead. I am the self-appointed care-taker of a deep past that absolutely no one in the next genera-tion or two, at least as far as I can see, has the slightest interest in. All signs of European peasant class are gone and they are American, with no felt connection to the people who carried these things along as far as they could. I, closer to the old-coun-try crowd in the family line, have always looked at those previous generations with a mixture of sorrow for their poverty and des-perate ambition, admiration for their courage to start a new life, and bewilderment that such humble folk figured they had any right to "conquer" land that for all time before them had resided in the domain of others. We are, so many of us Americans, the descendants of this particular combination of desperate, bold, and presumptuous.

Articles about downsizing will ask how many clothes you really need or suggest you get rid of the stack of magazines you'll never read. They don't address the sense of responsibility that keepers of family artifacts feel about the things holding our stories. In these stories lies an understanding of who we are, how we got here, and even where it's possible for us to go. The article writers reduce all this to an issue: clutter. If they do acknowledge objects passed on to us, they suggest we either pass these things on or get rid of them, as if "rid of them" were as easy as taking out the garbage. Maybe take a photo first with your phone, they tell us, put it in a file marked "Ancestors," and save to the Cloud.

On a practical level, in terms of space-saving, they may be right that it's possible to treasure our grandmother's wedding dress or Uncle Lew's World War II medals too much. But each of the objects we're holding onto reminds us of something that is not daily or routine but lives in some other part of our mental forest, over in the magic wood where the old ones gather and speak. I have let go of many, many items from the family and from my own life, as lots of my peers have done, whether or not they've read about the brown furniture or bothered to flip through countless magazine tips about downsizing. I can't say I miss what's gone.

Still, it seems to be getting harder, at least for me and maybe for many others, to release everything. All I can give as a reason is that I once loved running into my grandmother Martha's bedroom with news from the neighborhood and finding her bent over a drawer in the bureau searching for her hairbrush or a pair of wool gloves so that she could go hang clothes on the backyard line in cold weather. Or I might catch her lifting out a carefully pressed pillowcase embroidered by the sewing wizard among her daughters, my Aunt Marie, and slipping it over the feather pillow on her single bed. Living with her dresser keeps her with me. I loved her and I loved that whole hearty gang of people, descendants of Gudbrandsdalen and Oslo, desperate, bold, and presumptuous as they were.

My father, on the other hand, left me with few of his stories and none of his physical history other than his army cap (saved by my mother), his watch, and a short plank of weathered wood. The cap was passed on to me; the watch I slipped from his hand shortly after he died; I'd found the plank on my own.

Neither of my parents felt any compunction to save bits of their own past together. They'd moved around a lot in their younger years and quickly learned how to get rid of unnecessary possessions, and they were committed to order in all things. Their house in Iowa, especially in their old age, was tidy and minimalist. They kept photographs, but periodically even those collections were purged. All the furniture was modern and changed from time to time, old stuff recycled via Goodwill, released without sentiment. No objects from their distant past got in the way of their need for clear spaces and crisp lines.

I went searching one summer for my father's childhood ranch in North Dakota. With the help of his cousin, I arrived at the site of the two-story house I'd seen in photos. Made of fieldstone and rough lumber, it had given itself over to weather and lay now in a small pile, most of the lumber and stones reclaimed by the earth.

When I next traveled to Iowa and gave my father one short, dark piece of wood I'd salvaged from his former home (even a single field stone was too heavy to pack and carry with me), he stared at it. He did not touch the board fondly. He didn't touch it at all. He didn't launch into any stories about what it was like to live in a stone farmhouse built by his parents and their neighbors. He didn't describe treks to the nearby lake I'd spotted there and remember wild things that crept around it or flew overhead. He didn't speak a word for a while. Finally, he said, "What am I supposed to do with this?"

I quickly realized that this man was not going to hold a plank of wood from his past and become a storyteller at the age of sixty-seven. I also recognized how clueless I'd been about the fact some older people might want to divest themselves of belongings instead of add to the store.

As for my longing to know more about his early life, I'd have to be satisfied with the bits and pieces I could scrape together mostly from other people. But at least I'd seen the place where he'd grown up. Maybe he'd always disliked that ranch. Maybe he'd hoped that all those passing years would have given the earth time to swallow every last rock, nail, and board of his prairie home. I did know that the bank had reclaimed it during the great Depression and kicked his family out. Whatever had made me think a piece of wood from that sad history would please him? Still, I was pleased that I'd been to that place and touched it with mind, heart, hands.

Late in her life, my mother dropped one more tidbit about the bureau of my ancestors. She said that it had once supported a large mirror. I'm glad that mirror is gone now, so that I don't have to see my reflection as I approach those drawers each day, bracing myself for a wrestling match in order to grab a pair of socks, my face filled with both regard for the past and a longing to put something light and airy in this object's place, something with drawers that open willingly. But then, what would a brand-new piece of furniture like that have to tell me?

Today, with my father and my mother and their siblings, my siblings, and all of the old relatives gone, I recognize I may have gone overboard with this whole hanging-onto-stuff thing. But for many of us, a little sign pops up on the road to old age, pointing toward the family museum: *This way lay the stories.* Held within these stories, like codes, are the family legacies: the values, beliefs, cautions, aspirations, the character traits worth passing on and those best left behind. If we pay attention, we can still hear the guidance and encouragement of our ancestors in each telling, even if the telling is only to ourselves.

Despite what the well-meaning articles urge me to do, the dresser is mine for now. Mine to live with. Mine to die with. Mine to pass on to . . . no one. After I die, it could end up at a thrift store in nearby Scappoose, sitting outside by the door, a lingonberry- or- grape- or marionberry-decorated curiosity, its stubborn drawers permanently open to reveal knick-knacks, maybe even a few ceramic owls resembling those that had flown through the ancient forest from whence it came. A cardboard sign on top will describe which color tag on the goods inside the shop indicate 50 percent off for the day and which indicate the senior citizen 10 percent discount. Now and then a customer about to enter might imagine they hear the low moo of a cow or a tiny rattle coming from the old brown thing and stop to listen before deciding the wind is playing tricks. It will be the one store possession that can safely be left outside after closing, night after night, year in and year out, a sturdy Nordic guardian of the premises. No one will ever steal it.

Hair: The Thick and Thin of It

Early on during my first year of school, my mother cornered me in the bathroom every morning to deal with what she called my "bald spot," a birthmark according to the doctor who delivered me, a forceps injury according to her. My hair was thick and heavy except for this almost round, whitish patch at the crown. Its circumference was a little larger than a Ping-Pong ball. Nothing had ever sprouted there.

I fought those brushstrokes, pressing my body against the wall and sticking to it like a lizard. Usually a compliant child, I couldn't tolerate hair arranging, at least not the kind that took place in that room. Even though the bald area itself wasn't painful, I sometimes cried as a last resort when my mother finally maneuvered her way behind me and nudged me over to the mirror.

Crying changed nothing, but it felt justified anyway. I hated being fussed with, but my mother felt determined to get this thing concealed by using the masses of hair around it. Like a general at war, she deployed everything in her arsenal: barrettes, bobby pins, clips, rubber bands (no Scrunchies then, no colorful hair bands). Looking up at her anxious face in the bathroom mirror, I knew when she flushed with a glow of triumph that the ordeal had ended. She'd managed to keep the bald spot out of sight for one more day. Then, and only then, was I free to go.

I felt, to put it mildly, flawed. On the heads of my two older brothers generous amounts of hair covered every millimeter. They never found themselves in the bathroom poked with pins. The hair of other girls my age blew around in the breeze like fairy tresses, flew behind them as they pumped themselves higher and higher on the swings in the playground, bounced in the fresh air as they skipped or ran. My hair, clamped into submission with one or more devices, enjoyed no freedom of movement at all because something was wrong with my head.

Around this time, I saw my first movie, *Samson and Delilah*. In fact, I saw it three times because it cost only a nickel and my brother Michael, seven, possessed a small stack of nickels he'd won playing marbles. We went alone downtown to the Bismarck cinema each time; no parents or older brother came along to explain anything to us.

Seated in that dark theater, legs dangling far above the floor, I learned that a mysterious and great power, almost as big as God, lurks in hair. With a full head of it, Samson could bring down a building using only his bare hands; without it—thanks to Delilah—he was helpless. My heart went out to him. Delilah, played by Hedy Lamar, reminded me a bit of my mother.

After my first permanent at age nine, waves surrounded my face, while a clump of braid lay hog-tied over my scalp's major blight. By this time my mother no longer called it a bald spot. She referred to it simply as my "spot," as in, "Come here. Let me cover up your spot." By then my lizard days were over. I knew who held control over my hair.

Not long after the permanent, my parents got a loan from a relative and arranged a surgery to make the spot go away. (Later, they did the same thing with my "lazy" eye, but that's another story.) Early one morning, we left our small town for the big city, Minneapolis. I don't remember checking into the hospital, but I do remember that a man wheeled me on a white bed along a white hallway and into a white room. *Down, down, down* I sank under a mask of stinky gas held to my face by one of three women dressed head to foot in black. Pink faces hanging out of white frames looked down on me from a swoony distance. I knew what they were called, but I'd never encountered a nun before in real life, and I was pretty certain the spelling was *none*. I wondered if that meant they didn't actually exist. Maybe I'd been tricked and my spot had led me to death itself.

Later, when I woke up, another *none* entered my hospital room to take my temperature. Even though I hadn't died, I didn't like looking at her. I rolled my eyes upward and saw Jesus on a cross on the wall above my bed. I knew I should feel worse for what had happened to him than for my own sore head, but instead I felt we'd both been wronged.

Post-surgery a tight bandage was wrapped around my skull and stayed there for a long time, maybe weeks, I don't remember. Day followed day with that itchy white helmet in place. Underneath it, an infection brewed along the hairline of my forehead, directly above my right eye. This itched more than all the rest put together. I rubbed over and over at the stiff bandage, even though that didn't help.

My mother didn't guess there was an infection under there. When the bandage finally came off in the doctor's office, she was shocked to see that an ugly, boiling wound had formed. Nothing to worry about, claimed the doctor, just as honest as the one who'd wielded the forceps. This thing would scab over and be gone in no time, he said.

It did scab over and eventually left a scar. Although the surgery had reduced the spot's size a little, I turned ten with two areas on my head that could not grow hair, but at least the new one was smaller and could be easily hidden, my mother said, by bangs. She cut them herself.

Eventually I had the chance to govern my own hair. In college, I let it grow long and parted it in the middle, like so many other American college girl in the 1960s. I felt pleased that the sheer weight of all that hair covered the bald spot, and I could forget about it. By the time I graduated, I'd completely stopped checking the back of my head in the mornings with a hand mirror.

One day in my twenties, I gave myself a super short haircut. I wanted life to be easy and to be oblivious about my appearance. Oblivious worked, at least for a while. When I started getting jobs in offices as a temp, I found myself once again checking the spot every day. My hair had grown out slightly longer by then, but I knew the spot was still a problem because, amazingly, co-workers felt free to ask, "What's that thing on the back of your head?" I got very good at covering it up. My own look of triumph in the bathroom mirror replaced my mother's.

Over the years, I dealt with the area showing or not showing only intermittently. If, in some context or other, I felt bothered by questions and unwilling to tell the story, which sometimes included even the *nones* and the ether, I covered it up. The older I got, the more certain I became that one day the last shreds of vanity would fade away and I'd be free of any concern whatsoever. But I am, it turns out, my mother's daughter.

Around age sixty, at a hair salon, I learned about hair powder. I embraced it. If I felt a need to cover my spot—yes, I'd been calling it that in the quiet of my own mind for many years—I applied a little of the magical powder. The spot didn't disappear, but it sort of blended in. Then at seventy-five, a big change came.

My hair had gradually been thinning, as will happen to some of us as we grow older, but I'd started out with a lot of it and plenty of thickness remained, even after going gray. I won't say I found it easy to watch silver and white coming in to replace the dark shade of a lifetime, or that I shrugged at what this new shade whispered to me in the mirror about mortality, but at least it didn't surprise me. Massive hair loss that came out of the blue took me off guard. Most surprising and disheartening of all, the landscape of that already completely hairless area near the crown of my head changed. The bald spot began to spread. The powder couldn't cover it all without looking like, well, powder.

Everybody loses hair throughout the day. I'd noticed an increase in the normal amount around menopause, but then it settled down and the usual growth and shedding cycles returned and stayed for about twenty years. Although I'd expected my thick hair to thin somewhat as I aged, I didn't expect to watch strands fall from my scalp two by two, then five by five. For a while, I chalked it up to stress over COVID, but then ten by ten came along. Daily. Okay, I'm old, I thought, and I'm stressed, but how could this be right?

My mother had lost a significant amount of her hair by her nineties, but that loss came gradually. One day she decided to wear a wig and be done worrying about it. But I was seventy-five. (I want to say *only* seventy-five, but *only* a certain segment of people will understand what I mean by that, and they are all that age or beyond.)

I started to see hair everywhere—tangles of it on the shower floor and strands lying about on all the other floors and surfaces, including my clothes, the kitchen counter, couch, sheets, laptop, car. I was shedding like a cat in mid-July, but it was the middle of winter. It also happened to be the first winter of the pandemic. No vaccines existed yet. Driving to my doctor's office to ask her to look at my hair, of all things, felt trivial and also scary because of the elevator, waiting room, tiny exam room, the doctor herself.

I performed my own examinations. I watched as the part widened. Once hidden by layers of thickness, pink scalp peeped through a curtain of hair that grew thinner and thinner overall as the months passed. Not only had its willingness to stick with me for a lifetime come to an end, but my hair's natural heaviness and coarseness, something I'd alternately liked and fought with, altered. Robustness diminished until I woke one day a few months later and looked in the mirror to see that the majority of it had turned fine as spider silk.

After the vaccine released me from pandemic seclusion and I could get together with friends in safe ways, I noticed that many of them didn't comment on my hair loss. Women who'd been eager to discuss hair with me all of our adult lives, old and good friends, needed prompting, but when prompted they denied what I pointed to, finger to pinkening head. They reached out and touched my hair and told me this spider webby mess felt "silky and soft." They told me that losing hair when we're older is perfectly normal. *Looks great! You look great!*

I considered this friendly gaslighting, an attempt to make me feel better. It may have been intended as kind, but I'd been alone with this issue and needed more.

I tried again, using science. I explained that, instead of the normal 75 to 100 strands of hair that drop from human heads all over the this earth each day, I was losing 150 to 200 per day, a category different from normal, even *old* normal. This fact helped them understand my concern, but I still felt a little embarrassed to say that I was finally going to consult a dermatologist about it.

The dermatologist said my hair loss was not related to age. The scalp was inflamed, so some kind of dermatitis may be contributing to it, along with the fact that I'd been vegan and gluten free for almost a year. She asked what I ate and pronounced it alarmingly low in protein. We discussed stress: the pandemic, the nail-biting presidential election, the nail-biting presidential election aftermath. Hair can't thrive with intense stress. Also, living in rainy Oregon apparently didn't help. I'd spent way too many days inside for the past year. My Vitamin D levels had plummeted from previous annual exam numbers. High stress, low vitamin D, low protein—she didn't like the sound of any of it.

About the spot the doctor said little; about nearby hairless areas, small lakes and rivers of pink, she used the word "destruction." She numbed my head and cut out a tiny portion of scalp to see if some underlying condition might be the culprit. I stayed calm as I could under the knife, trying to prepare myself for head scar number three.

As I sat on the short stool she provided for the micro-surgery, I considered this case of destruction—similar to what Delilah did to Samson when she'd chopped off his beautiful black hair, only maybe I'd done it to myself, with a little help from the times we were in and a naturopath who, before the pandemic started, had recommended a vegan and gluten-free diet but neglected to tell me what to eat. Fair enough. She didn't know me. Unless it's prepared by someone else who knows and cares about what they're doing, I'm so uninterested in cooking and food that it never occurred to me to keep track of protein intake.

The young dermatologist sewed up my scalp and gave me instructions about how to treat this new wound. Throughout the visit, she had not treated me condescendingly, as so many doctors treat women my age. She gave meaning to the phrase uttered by medical office workers since the medical profession started: "The doctor will see you now." In that exam room, for the first time in many months, I felt seen.

Dr. —— talked about products to pour on my head morning after morning for all the rest of my days to possibly regrow hair. Given some of the side effects, I did not feel anxious to try them.

She sent me home with diet and shampoo instructions, along with a follow-up date to put on my calendar.

As I walked out into the hallway, I thought, "Alice would approve this visit." My mother had been gone for five years at that point, and I felt such a pang of longing for her, remembering a conversation during the time she lived in an assisted living facility nearby. In her nineties, pre-wig, she stood in front of her bathroom mirror one morning combing her hair and growing increasingly frustrated. I stood behind her, checking areas in the back, trying to help. She told me she had to spread around the small amount of white hair she had left to cover all the visible patches of scalp.

"But nothing works anymore," she said. "I start to feel sorry for myself and then I think of what you've had to put up with all your life." She shook her head sympathetically and her eyes met mine in the mirror.

Stories, even those told over and over again through decades, can take unlikely turns when new information comes in. Some statement or other spurs new growth, and there you are, momentarily disoriented and then more clear-minded about yourself and others near and dear to you than you ever thought possible. The bathroom struggle had once been a go-to story to explain what I meant when I said that my mother and I didn't get along. As soon as I could, I'd chosen to live far away from her, but her move to Portland to live near me in her old age changed everything. It had provided us with the chance to heal our uncomfortable differences, and we'd taken full advantage of it.

We'd already made great strides in accepting one another when we sat down together that morning, she in the recliner and I on the sofa. We talked about how we both saw that long-ago bathroom as the starting point of a contentious relationship. She had her version of what she saw in the bathroom mirror—I was impossible—and I had mine—she was controlling. Each of us had heard the other tell her version a few times to various people over the years, but now she told a piece of the story I'd never known. She explained to me how the hair fights in the bathroom began.

One day not long after I'd started first grade, she noticed I'd begun wearing my brother Michael's Cub Scout beanie to school. She asked why and apparently—I have no memory of this—I'd told her that other children had been teasing me about the area of missing hair; if I wore the beanie they didn't tease me. That's when she'd become determined to cover it herself, to protect her little girl from bullying.

From my perspective, I explained as we sat together, all that twisting and poking had felt like torture. I'd thought she was trying to fix some awful mistake in me. Because I didn't recall saying anything to her about being teased, I had no idea she'd been determined to thwart the bullies.

I sighed, and so did she. An early injury between us had healed. A conversation like this one would have helped us greatly when I was five and resigned to wearing a beanie for the rest of my life and she was thirty-five and dead set against it. But we didn't have conversations like that in the 1950s. If a spaceship had landed and an extraterrestrial walked directly to our house to tell us *communication really does matter*, it would not have put a dent in this norm.

I thought of my mother's protectiveness a few years ago when I rescued a cat from a situation in which she was constantly either ignored or grabbed at. What broke my heart at first sight was that her coat was dull and she'd started tearing out her own fur, leaving whitish patches of skin exposed. Once Riley had been living at my house for a while, her stress fell away. She stopped chewing at the fur. Here, she could be her powerful, settled self.

Eventually, her fur grew back and became overall much healthier. Without chunks of it missing, she looked confident as any cat can be, and I think she felt restored. Samson may have been the first person who demonstrated that it is far from shallow to be concerned about hair, a matter of life or death for him, but Riley's life didn't depend on her fur. She prefers having it, that's all. She likes to zone out and groom it, eyes half closed in bliss.

Hair isn't a life-or-death matter for me either, but why should we expect women, after a lifetime of hair conversations and experiences, to simply not care about it once past a certain age? Why not care? In some ways, we might care even more than ever because we're older now, and our hair, what we have left of it, is infused with meaning and history. We can think about, and spend time on, lots of challenges, including the environment, hunger, domestic terrorism and violence, a global pandemic—all manner of things that affect us—*and* we can, if we want, also spare a few moments to consider our hair. After all, younger women, even those the most committed to changing things for the better, still consider theirs.

Yet, I've had conversations with many women well over sixty who can discuss at length some aspect of their hair before sheepishly closing down the conversation with, "Oh, it's only hair, isn't it? I'm older now. It's not important." This sentence marks the end of every conversation with woman after woman in my life. The same people who have just talked about how much they care will suddenly want to dismiss the subject. It is probably not how women with hypotrichosis, or total baldness from birth on, would end a conversation about hair, young or old. Even after dealing with only one small spot of baldness all my life, I can't end a conversation about hair with a shrug and dismissal of its importance to me.

Both sudden loss or hair drifting away at a slower pace are

fraught for almost anyone, regardless of age. When I began to lose the hair around the spot so that areas of baldness spread across the top of my head, no longer confined to what had been my normal, post-surgery, slightly-less-than-Ping-Pong-ball size, I felt compassion for all bald or balding men and women on the planet—unintentionally bald, that is—at least the ones who cared about such things.

I'm eating more protein, per Dr. —'s orders. I take Vitamin D and de-stress daily with walks, photography, and drawing. No matter what I do, though, I'm old now, so sooner rather than later, my whole body, not only my hair, will be leaving me stranded somewhere—or nowhere. (Only the *nones* may know for sure, though I doubt it.)

In the meantime, there's a lot going on and there's also hair: hair thinning, hair lost, and sometimes—maybe, who knows?—a little hair regained. I don't know what will happen with mine. If I live long enough, eventually most of it will probably fall out, and I'll be like the Velveteen Rabbit, or possibly like my mother, which is okay, too. Either way, I believe that the child who sat with her brother in that movie theater all those years ago and concluded that a mysterious power lurks in hair was right. I'll miss it when it's gone.

Where Are We Now?

When she reached her mid-nineties, my mother began asking a lot of scientific questions: Why is the sky blue? What's inside of a cloud? How does that crow over there pecking at a McDonald's French fry dropped on the side of the road recognize such a thing as food? How is it that, as trees grow taller, both sides stay balanced? Alice was trying to catch up on things never taught at the small prairie town school she'd attended, or maybe she had never thought to ask about as she passed through her life in a series of midwestern towns while raising children, keeping house, and now and then working as a telephone operator or in a dress shop.

Once she entered her nineties and settled in near me here in Portland, all barriers to seeking knowledge fell away. If she asked a question and I didn't know the answer, which happened quite a lot, we tried to find out together. Her curiosity fed mine, and I became aware that something happens as we grow older. Unless a person is extremely foolish or just not paying attention, she will stop taking things for granted, including the physical world, the very world, she realizes, that she is not so deeply rooted in after all, a place she'll be leaving before too long. What is this place? And how *does* that crow know that a French fry is for eating?

Reawakened curiosity and searching for a new life direction are two reasons more and more people over the age of sixty are enrolling in college classes, often for free or reduced rate. When she was in her late seventies, my friend Eleanor drove across town to sit in on French classes at Portland State University for a couple of years. She'd always wanted to improve her French and she finally had time to do it. All states offer an opportunity, once you reach a certain age, to take classes at low cost. If someone is isolated for health reasons, can't drive, has no public transport budget, or is simply too busy to go to a classroom but has access to a computer, they can search for online courses. Coursera gives free online courses in anything from Buddhism to activism to dinosaurs, without exams unless you want to take them. When in her sixties, another friend, Ruth, took a seminar on modern poetry taught by Al Filreis, director of the University of Pennsylvania's Kelly Writers House, through Coursera. She said she felt like she was in a classroom: smart young people, a good teacher, pop quizzes, and lots of optional reading.

Back in the 1990s, Alice had welcomed Google as the Oracle of Delphi. She used it mostly to win arguments with my father. Even after he'd died and she moved here, with eyesight failing and a loss of finger dexterity, she was still able to google things, and she looked up whatever struck her as interesting. She researched everything from the location of the Garden of Eden to the distance from the earth to the moon. For her, the Internet was a resource and a pleasure. Based on my mother's experience and that of many of the people at her assisted living facility, along with my own experience and that of my friends, the techno-averse elder is a myth.

Through Alice's last years, she continued to ask me questions. Sometimes she turned from scientific inquiries to philosophical ones, including an ongoing inquiry about death. This began to drift into her conversations casually and unexpectedly, like a regular visitor who spent most of his time reading in the hall but now and then passed through on the way to the kitchen to get a cup of coffee or make some toast. She tried to look at things squarely but admitted she was puzzled. In conversations about those we'd lost in our immediate and extended family, which was almost everyone by the time she neared one hundred years old, she once shook her head and asked, "Where *are* they?" She did not have religion, as the expression from her era goes. She'd never been interested in a formal structure that would tell her what to believe and what to cast aside, but from time to time she did say, "There's something. I can't call it God but there's *something*."

She began to use the word "precious" more and more frequently. If I brought her a rose, she'd look at it, lightly touch the petals, and declare the flower precious. I was precious, as were all my friends who came by for visits. Some of the aides at the assisted living facility were precious, as well as a fellow resident with whom she'd become friends, her dining partner, Irene, who lived to 110.

When they'd first met, Irene was 105. She and Alice told each other stories about their five sisters, Irene's were long gone; at the time, Alice had only one living sister, Pearl. Although she and Pearl argued about politics, she still found her sister precious. One day a tree outside her window, to which she had recited a poem she'd learned in childhood, "Trees" by Joyce Kilmer, shimmied in a flutter of leaves top to bottom the moment she spoke the poem's last word. This mysterious dance, too, she later described to me as precious.

I listened as that word gained momentum in her vocabulary, casting its net and catching hold of her world. This earth, its plants and animals and birds and various human members, its scientific facts and strange occurrences, all were precious in the truest sense, that is, they were of exquisite value to her.

It's never too late to ask where, exactly, we are and what we're going to look into while we're here. I received that wisdom from my mother and I'm trying to hang onto it in old age as I ask my own questions. What a lot there is to gather close and hold as lightly as possible, while exercising the maximum amount of curiosity and appreciation.

PART TWO

There Was
an Old Woman

There was an old woman toss'd up in a basket
Nineteen times as high as the moon;
Where she was going I couldn't but ask it,
For in her hand she carried a broom.

"Old woman, old woman, old woman," quoth I,
"O whither, O whither, O whither, so high?"
"To brush the cobwebs off the sky!"
"Shall I go with thee?" "Aye, by-and-by."

—NURSERY RHYME

There Was an Old Woman

Aunt Mattie introduced me to the Old Woman. Every day at 6 p.m., Mattie walked fifteen blocks home from her job in the children's department at the library carrying picture books for us to read together. I would hop around near the front door waiting for her, excitement increasing at the first glimpse of her arms burdened with books and jubilant when she finally came inside and shrugged off her coat. At last she'd sit down in my grandmother's big cushioned chair, ready for me to crawl into her lap. The wide, colorful pages turned: *The Runaway Bunny*, *Winnie the Pooh*, *The Tale of Peter Rabbit*, *Make Way for Ducklings*, *Horton Hatches the Egg*, and many rhymes and tales in which the Old Woman appeared.

The Old Woman was usually poor, and her looks ranged anywhere from dowdy to downright hideous. One old woman with a lot of children lived in a shoe, and she was so mean she spanked each child before putting them to bed. The rest were childless and lived alone in a faraway place, and these were dangerous people of a different order. I met the Old Woman in the gingerbread house who tries to shove Hansel and Gretel into her oven; the Sea Witch who lives in a house made of the bones of shipwrecked men and takes the little mermaid's voice in payment for a pair of legs; the Evil Queen in disguise who offers a poisoned apple to her stepdaughter; the wicked fairy godmother who casts a spell on a princess so she'll prick her finger on a spindle and fall into deep sleep; Baba Yaga, who stalks around the forest on chicken legs; a wicked sorceress who locks Rapunzel in a tower.

Sometimes she had a name: Old Mother Hubbard didn't have a bone for her dog; Old Mother Goose flew to the moon on the back of a gander. Often, though, the Old Woman was nameless, and when she set out to do harm it was harm to children, from spanking for no reason to attempted murder. Even when these people were helpful, such as the gift-giving three hags in *East of the Sun, West of the Moon*, it was hard for an innocent heart to feel anything but repulsion.

While my aunt read to me, my grandmother, the only real old woman in my life, worked nearby in the kitchen cooking dinner and filling the house with the aroma of fresh bread—and not a single child—baking in her oven. She was not ugly. She did not live in a hut by herself. She was an important member of a crowded house, where no one ever called her "the old woman." An extended family lived with her: two of her six daughters, Mattie and my mother, along with my father, my two brothers, and me, the youngest at the time. My mother and aunt called her Mama. My father called her Martha. To Bruce, Michael, and me, she was Grandma.

Never once did my grandmother put down her rolling pin and wander into the living room while Mattie read me a picture book showing some hateful witch with a waterfall of moles tumbling down her long nose and say, "You know this isn't what real old women are like, right? I'm one, for example." If she paid any attention at all to the stories, which she could easily overhear in our small house, she didn't comment on these fellow members of her gender and age group when they popped into plots and tried to ruin some child's life. I imagine she thought of the books as interesting stories filled with color and caution, which they were.

Both subtly and not so subtly, many fairy tales used fear to manipulate children into what was considered acceptable behavior. They warned against going past prescribed boundaries, including moral boundaries, and they described consequences for disobeying or transgressing that were harrowing. Through the Brothers Grimm, these stories came into popularity with adults first, and then were shared with children. My grandmother wasn't a fearsome person at all, but she'd been born in the late 1800s and probably saw nothing wrong with this theory of training, though she was ever gentle with us.

Even though I knew she was old, I didn't ever think of my grandmother as remotely like the Old Woman I met in the books. I might have considered her at least a little bit magical had I known some of the fabulous stories, a few with fairy tale dimensions, that were attached to her life. For example, when she was a young mother, she fell into an icy well and managed to claw her way up the cold and slippery walls and out again because she had to get back to her children in the farmhouse. There's a tale as chilling (in more ways than one) as a stepmother/witch handing a girl a poisoned apple.

But I didn't hear my grandmother's account of once upon a time being young and falling into a well until I was older. Like most small children, I assumed grandparents were born old. You enter a life in which you play, eat, splash around in puddles, run barefoot in summer, learn new things all the time, and talk to people called grandparents who are just there, onstage already, along with everybody else you know.

Of all the big people in the house, I felt closest to Mattie and my grandmother. Mattie was the third of Martha's six daughters, the only unmarried one, a saver who loaned all the others money when they needed it. Her closest friends were her fellow librarians. Her life was books, both at home and at work. She borrowed abundantly from the library. In her single bed, she sat up late on crisp white sheets that my grandmother had pushed and pulled through a wringer washing machine, rinsed in bluing, hung in sweet prairie breezes to dry, and then ironed. Tucked into her starched, white bedtime cocoon, my aunt read novels, biographies, poetry, and mysteries.

Mattie, my mother, and my grandmother tried their best to make the scrub of pale brown dirt outside our house—an army barracks sold at auction they'd had trucked over to Bismarck from Mandan—into something that didn't remind them of the poverty they came from. One night under a full moon the three of them prepared the ground and walked around the yard scattering grass seed, which obediently grew into a state that Mattie could mow, tidy row after tidy row, until it resembled a well-behaved lawn. She loved quality things, especially clothes, but—ever mindful of her sisters' and their children's needs—spent her salary on herself sparingly: one coat, a soft blend of fine wool; a few well-made dresses for work; a black felt pillbox hat; a pancake-sized folding mirror with brass hinges and covered in flowery satin; a single gold cashmere sweater. I would sometimes stand on a chair and pull open the top drawer of her bureau so that I could feel the soft red leather of her coin purse squish between my fingers, press my nose against the scented soaps she'd tucked between the bright, filmy silk squares that she tied around her neck when she went to work, and count the brown paper-encased rolls of pennies, nickels, dimes, and quarters she saved. Occasionally, I opened a small blue paper book with rows of numbers. She'd told me the book was from the bank and listed her payments on the house we all lived in, each payment stamped in black ink. She accepted rent from my parents, but she depended on no one but herself.

Mattie was in her thirties when she read to me and sometimes referred to herself as an old maid, then laughed in a way that made me think being an old maid must be kind of funny and wonderful. Although my aunt dated men from time to time, it didn't seem like she'd ever want to marry anyone. Later, when I heard the term used in a derogatory way and saw a sour and pinched woman depicted as the Old Maid in a children's card game, I'd felt surprised and a little confused. Did people not realize how fine it was to be one?

Mattie read stories to me three decades before Bruno Bettelheim wrote *The Uses of Enchantment: The Meaning and Importance of Fairy Tales*, and more than half a century before Dr. Maria Tartar at Harvard started to question the ways the stories tried to control children in some of her books, such as *Off with Their Heads: Tales of the Culture of Childhood*. In our time, Mattie and I were free-ranging reader and listener. We might read *The Little Red Hen* and then *Hansel and Gretel* and then some nursery rhymes, all in a single sitting.

Nobody, including Mattie, separated the scary old woman from the grandmother for me, but I easily saw the differences. While hags and witches populated several stories, grandmothers were rare. When a grandmother did appear, she was on the same side as the child, not in opposition, but she played only a supporting role, nothing like the role my grandmother played in our house.

One storybook grandmother who got a fair-sized part to play belonged to *Little Red Riding Hood*, and I thought she'd been silly. She'd let the wolf in her door, and then couldn't handle anything about the situation after that, whereas I'd seen my grandmother decapitate a snake in our backyard with her hoe, tend her vegetable garden (same hoe), pluck a couple of chickens, wash pounds of family laundry on the wringer washer in the basement and hang it outside with wooden pins, cook up a tableful of food, and bake bread and heaping plates of cinnamon rolls all on the same day. Had a murderous wolf come to the door wanting to eat us, she would have taken care of that state of affairs right away. No time for nonsense.

Whatever the Old Woman might have been up to all day long in her faraway house, I had no idea. She was out there somewhere in the woods, where she probably mucked about on her lonesome until some children she could scare the bejesus out of stumbled by.

I never asked Mattie if witches were real as I sat on her lap looking at the pictures while she read, nor did she offer anything along the lines of, "My dear little niece person, here we have representations of the Dark Feminine, an archetype sometimes used to represent a force we own as women, a force that contains wisdom, ferocity, mutability, and skill. However, a long-term patriarchal overcast has turned all that into the witch you see in these tales and, thanks to that, she is evil and unsightly more often than not."

No. None of that. Mattie had been the child of impoverished parents and educated in a school in a town of three hundred people. She worked in the Bismarck library out of pure enthrallment with books and the courage to show up there one day and ask for a job. She had no money to pursue a degree, let alone pass through any studies of mysticism, feminism, and Carl Jung, even though all would have fascinated her.

I was the child of a white, lower-middle-class American household. My father sold shoes in a department store; my mother worked as a telephone operator. I lived in a house filled with descendants of northern Europeans. No one mentioned that I was encountering a *type* when I met the old women on the pages of children's books. If you are a peer reading this, regardless of your background you know that American kids from other classes and descended from other countries and cultures met the same type, given that no US press back then would have considered publishing a variety of cultural viewpoints on anything, let alone old age. Together, whole generations of us encountered the old—and particularly the Old Woman—as poor, ragged, alone, and often creepy.

And so I met the Old Woman as presented and accepted her as real because children don't make distinctions between fiction and nonfiction. Read children a few books with monsters as characters and pretty soon they're looking for monsters under their own beds. Read a child some books about witches and pretty soon she might have a nightmare about such a person coming for her. It happened to me: *I'm four years old and standing in the living room of our house. The prairie darkness outside is moonless and deep, and I look out at it through a sheer fiberglass curtain and watch as a witch flies by, over and over. She is dressed in black and circling the house. Her features aren't clear but I know her face is old, very old. She is swift in her circling, ever closer, soundless. I am silent, too. Awestruck. But surely I'm not the only one who sees her. In one corner of the room, a lamp glows with yellow light. I turn and look to see who from this crowded household is here with me, but no one is with me. The circling witch, the gauzy window, the terrible night and I are alone together. I am terrified.*

Time passed and, with it, my childhood. I remembered the nightmare through the years, but never gave much thought to the old being old, men or women, and how they and those of us in my generation and everybody else carried with us, and unconsciously drew from, negative images of old age. Thanks to a culture that generally holds older adults in low esteem, negativity was unavoidable. It came not only from popular culture—TV and magazines—but even from the supposedly higher arts of literature, theater, music, and film.

Recently, though, I began reading about the misunderstandings and stereotypes around this time of life and the sometimes appalling mistreatment that comes in their wake. I came across the term "the elder within" used by a well-known author on aging, Ken Dychtwald, and it made me start to think about the elder within me and how she had been formed and faring as I traveled this long road.

It occurred to me that the Old Woman in those picture books had become part of me. Pooh and Horton and Peter Rabbit and all the loveable and childlike characters had become part of me once, too, but they had left with childhood. Now, as I entered old age myself, it became clearer each day that my first impressions of the Old Woman hadn't gone anywhere. No waterfall of moles cascaded down a long, long nose, but the same recessed eyes with bags below, the kind that had once, as a little girl, made me squirm with discomfort, now looked back at me from the mirror. If I get into a spat with a bristly young guy over a parking spot, he might shout at me, "Get out of my way, Old Woman!" If I show up as a nameless stranger in someone else's conversation about me, I'll most likely be referred to by my new generic name.

I'm determined never to joke about my age to cover forgetfulness the way some people do, and I decided a while back that I'd try to always look at my face in the mirror when brushing my teeth, even if there are days it makes me uncomfortable. Well and good, but the Old Woman still needs to be addressed when she shows up as the default version of me in my own unconscious, even if I can't do anything about how she lives in the unconscious minds of millions of others.

I thought about the fairy tales and folk tales read to me, all of them passed down by people from villages in northern Europe hundreds of years ago, making their way into the stories of Charles Perrault and into the mind and memory of Dorothea Viehmann.

From her memories and from others, they poured out into the notebooks of the Brothers Grimm. Even if they'd been drawing on some ancient understandings of gender and power, many of them carried on the notion of the "difficult" old female. The Old Woman was scooped up and dutifully collected by the folklorists and created such an impression that it's hard to this day to let go of her. Little girls still come to the door on Halloween dressed as witches. "Witch" is still a curse hurled at women. In fact, women are still arrested for practicing witchcraft in some countries, and an awful lot of these women are old, poor, and marginalized. They are scapegoats, not practitioners of magic and mayhem.

The stories were old long before anyone transcribed them. None of them were invented by villagers on the spot. They carried certain codes for behavior in society, and these were passed down through generations. In the case of the Old Woman, children received the message that there was something if not outright repugnant, then at least suspect about her. In every rhyme or telling of a story about a witch or sorceress or evil queen or any other dilapidated female figure of menace, fear of the Old Woman was reinforced.

But who, I wondered, would these misfits have been in those long-ago days? Who were the stories based on, if anyone? Maybe the witch was the woman who could never bear a child and so her husband abandoned her; the one who was beaten by her husband or parents or grown children and ran away to live alone on the outskirts of the village; the one who was left a widow; the spinster; the lesbian. With all the time she had to herself and no need to mediate in families or compromise in arguments, maybe she'd held fast to her own point of view, kept a serious eye on nature, and invited animals close for companionship, focusing on them in ways the married and more privileged women found foolish, strange, even frightening. When she grew old, she was not the grandmother close to the hearth. She grew old alone. But how, the other villagers may have questioned, can a childless woman manage this? How does she do without grandchildren? What to make of such a person?

It would have been hard not to make a lot of her. People like to make things up about those who aren't like them. Think about her for even a little while and wonder how on earth she got along by herself with no man and no children to make her life more comfortable. Surely she must feel jealous of those who had both. Likely she'd wanted children, too, but missed out. Poor thing. Let's tell a tale or two or ten about her. Make her a witch!

According to two writers on the topic of children's relationship to ageism, Donna Couper and Fran Pratt (*Learning for a Longer Life*), children can begin expressing ageist thoughts even at the age of three, and the negativity only increases over time. While they may think family members past a certain age in their own lives are completely fine, as I did, children absorb the culture's stereotypes of the old, including those found in children's literature. When asked if they wanted to be old, the children studied often answered no. Yet, the authors make clear, that future as an older person, if they're lucky, is waiting for them and they need to know about it. Many of us are aunts, great-aunts, and grandmothers. If we behave like the adults before us, who must have imbibed some magic elixir served in a tall glass of time to make them forget to discuss their aging process with us, and if we do not question the cultural stereotypes, we are doing the very young a disservice.

To the degree the old have been marginalized in our own thoughts, to the degree we haven't respected them as we've met them in our lives, and to the degree we continue to fear and reject them no matter where they arise, even in our own faces and bodies, we will suffer as we become older adults ourselves. Some suffering around this is unavoidable, given the culture, given the human body. But some of it we can transform by being exactly who we want to be. Both The Old Woman and The Old Man within are going to insist on that, anyway. And some of that suffering can be gently met in consciousness, too. Many conclusions we arrived at so innocently, even while safe in the arms of a loving family, were wrong.

We have two choices: to let children discover the old in stories and explain nothing—not even the fact that they will also be old one day and that we are all growing older—or talk to them about aging. If we choose the second path, we can help them find ways to protect their future personhood, their "elder within," in the same way that many of us diligently took the time, in therapy and other ways, to go back and protect our small selves by acknowledging and nurturing the "inner child."

Throughout her life, long before and long after my grandmother died, even as she grew very old herself and even in the dead of winter, Mattie would step out onto her back steps and greet the moon's ascent into the night sky. But then, she'd always been the odd one: the only sister of six never to marry, the smartest one, the one with her own money and with a will so strong her sisters would heel to it throughout their own long lives. Why wouldn't she worship the moon?

In another time, another village, Mattie might have fallen into both "old maid" and "witch" territory, but in her village, Bismarck, she drew devoted admirers, not a damning crowd. I learned this when she, in her eighties, and I, in my fifties, began spending a couple of weeks together at her house every summer.

Whenever I'd take her to the dentist, the doctor, the Red Cross station where she'd been giving blood regularly since World War

II, the now grown people who had known her as their children's librarian talked to her about missing the German cuckoo clock in the old Carnegie library or certain stories they remembered her reading to them at Saturday story hour. They asked about the books she was reading.

I visited her in that same house where once, long ago, we had lived together. An army barracks converted into a home might sound like a large place, but it was actually built to hold only a few German prisoners of war. Each room was small.

Despite its diminutive size, which I could now see must have been an incredibly tight fit for the lot of us, the house had become a family museum and an archive of family history. Mattie wanted me to help her try to organize her things, especially her papers, and clean out no-longer-wanted items. We read old letters, sorted photographs of immigrant ancestors, paged through books, including some of the fairy tale books she'd read to me, which she'd brought home one by one as they were withdrawn, due to wear and tear, from the public library. We read over genealogies and edited family stories she'd written down.

During her eighty-sixth summer, Mattie and I sat one night in her living room, I on the floor and she in her softly cushioned chair, much like my grandmother's chair, where she'd once read to me. The night was hot, close, and quiet behind the sixth or seventh set of filmy white curtains that had spanned the three living room windows over the past fifty-some years.

Photographs were strewn on the floor all around us and more filled a shoebox on her lap. She showed me a picture of a group of several adults standing outside together in what looked like a clearing in a forest. The majority were young people, maybe in their twenties or thirties. Their clothing looked European, from the 1940s, and several of the women closely resembled one another.

Most of these people were either smiling or outright laughing. Even a fox terrier that one young woman held looked like he'd just heard a hilarious joke. In fact, everybody in the photograph looked pleased to be there and to be together. A grandmother with an easy smile stood among them.

"Those are my cousins who stayed in Norway," Mattie said, pointing to the younger members of the group. "That's Mama's side of the family." I was taken aback. Norwegian cousins who had decided not to emigrate to America and yet stayed in touch, at least for a while, with the American branch shouldn't have surprised me. But I'd never heard of them. Mattie said the photo had been taken during the war, meaning World War II.

She pondered the picture for a minute and then announced that she felt happy with her life, maybe happier than she'd ever been. Neither of us commented on her announcement; it felt true, and one of the happiest features of my own life was that she was still in it. We went on to pull more photographs from the shoebox.

Back home again, when I mentioned Mattie's comment to a friend, she said, "That's kind of remarkable." And I saw that it was. The reality of my own years piling up was settling in and I felt comforted to think there was more to aging than I'd imagined. Ironically, I learned this from the very person who had brought the scary old woman into my consciousness.

Mattie, my grandmother and my own mother, who lived to be one hundred, and all my other aunts and old relatives, are gone, and now I am the Old Woman. I don't live in a hut but in a house-boat on a river that flows along the edge of a forest. Many children have passed by my door and through my life and, like my grandmother, I haven't baked a single one of them. I have good neighbors. Most of my contemporaries, as opposed to those in the era of the Grimm brothers, are more accepting of spinsters, lesbians, widows, and abandoned women, at least for the moment. My sheets are *never* ironed, but I do climb into bed at night and, like Mattie, lose myself in a book.

Now I can see what I couldn't see clearly before. We don't turn into someone else when we become old. We don't swap out our passports and enter some other state. We bring our whole selves with us into old age, the same selves our bodies have carried all the way through our lives. Old shouldn't come as a surprise any more than the sunrise comes as a surprise. Who we become in old age is the elder within who finally manifests.

I rarely have bad dreams, but when I do, I sometimes think back to that first nightmare of so long ago. I remember standing at the window, watching the witch circling the house. I'd been born only four years before into a world where anything could happen. I was one of the lucky ones whose father came back from the war, which I knew nothing about during those years I sat on Mattie's lap and looked at books. Being alive and little was safe. I had no worries. But I did have the daunting task of trying to use everything I had to understand and draw in the fullness of human life, all that was commonplace, all that was mystery. I had to pull every part into me—my own grandmother and the Old Woman, the delight in a rhyme about a twinkling star, the shadows in a room where a soft finger is pricked by a spindle, cinnamon rolls and prairie grass, loving voices, decapitated snakes, white sheets on a clothesline; the wide variety of bright and dark that life contains. And all the unexpected help that comes! The wonder of a godmother who might draw up to your house in a pumpkin carriage, the kinship you can feel with a bear who lets you ride on his back, the closeness of a sibling who helps you drop bread crumbs along the way, whatever the way might be.

All the old stories have a beginning, middle, and end, a pattern copied from human, animal, and plant life. Now, more than ever, this reliable pattern brings time and the value of my own life within its boundaries into sharp focus. I don't want to waste the chapters that lead to the ending worrying about what they might contain or fighting it. Some of life now is fear-worthy, it's true, but when I look back I can see that's been true about life all along. I want to live this last part of my story well—the light, the shadows, and the magic of it. If the witch comes by, I want to fling aside the curtains, reach through the window into the darkness, and grasp her withered hand. With luck, she'll take me with her and show me new ways to see and new ways to be an old woman.

The Inside of Old

In a century-old Carnegie library that housed and sold retired library books, I once paid a dollar for a small volume of essays that became more and more meaningful to me as the years passed. *My Day*, by Jean Rhys, sat on a shelf beneath abundant light from one of the tall, arched windows, but a crowd of Anne Rice vampire novels overshadowed it; if its narrow spine had not been white, contrasting with the bright colors that filled the rest of the shelf, I would have passed right by. Three miniature essays make up this five-by-seven-inch book. I thought I knew about all of Rhys's work, but I'd never heard of *My Day*.

Jean Rhys wrote her great novel, *Wide Sargasso Sea*, over a span of years, many of them late in her life. She was seventy-six when she published that passionate backstory of the woman locked in the attic of Thornfield Hall in *Jane Eyre*. I checked the publication date on *My Day*: 1975. She was eighty-five. When I took the book home and read it all those years ago, it was the first time anyone had spoken to me in such a way—from a novel, essay or otherwise—on a topic never brought up in polite company: What does it feel like to be living inside of old age?

Here in this little book was a voice, and the voice of a great writer at that, describing in prose as clear as the waters of her birthplace, Dominica, what it was like to grow old in what she called the "ramshackle" house she occupied in Devon: ". . . age seldom arrives smoothly or quickly. It's more often a succession of jerks. After the first you slowly recover. You 'learn to live' with the consequences. Then comes another and another."

The first in this succession to notify me of the arrival of my own old age came well over a decade after reading those words. I stood in a long grocery line, my cart piled with goods I'd thought I needed when traveling the aisles, but which now looked mostly nonessential after all. My lower back hurt, but that had been happening off and on since I turned forty. The difference that day was that I couldn't manage to adjust myself so that I could stand comfortably, and I felt a low growl of impatience mounting inside as the line barely crawled forward. I fantasized about pushing the cart back into one of the aisles, leaving it there, and walking away.

But I stayed the course, even though I began to think of us all as ants nudging our finds slowly back toward the nest. I mentally ticked through what would come next: inch by slow inch forward, finally the conveyer belt, bag filling, payment, cart to car, drive a slow mile to bridge (rush hour; should have planned better), bumper to bumper on highway toward home, and finally into the moorage parking lot. But that wasn't the end of it. I'd still need to unload the goods from the car and place them into the cart that I'd thankfully had the foresight to leave near the recycling center instead of on my deck, and then *down down down* cart and I would go to my houseboat at the bottom of a steep, eighty-foot-long ramp where I'd unload everything again and would need to put it all away before I could sit, stare at the river, and simply go blank. I wanted that blankness so much that the desire for it almost hurt. Only a month or so before, I'd turned sixty-four.

※ ※ ※

Would I have applied the word *old* to describe what I felt and longed for back then? Did I even remember what Jean Rhys wrote at that moment? Probably not. But now that I've had ten more years of experience in the Long Life Department, I've thought of that day and her words, along with others in *My Day*, many times. The desire to sit in a state of blankness, or utter calm, began to stir within me more frequently, the way thoughts of an early morning swim at the YWCA once called to me, or a run on the beach, or a party. Wanting only to *be* became familiar as air. All those other things sometimes still call to me, but so rarely that when I do hear one of them it's like the voice of a stranger standing at my shoulder, startling me into asking, *What?*

Even if I'd had the word *old* on the tip of my tongue and wasn't afraid to place it directly onto my experience that day at the grocery store, how would I have expressed it? Could I have turned to the younger person behind me and announced, with some surprise, "You know what? I think I might be feeling kind of . . . old." They would have probably looked me up and down and then stared straight into my lined face and said, "And you're surprised at this because . . .?"

Of course even I, an outgoing person when in department stores, grocery stores, airports, or my own neighborhood, wouldn't have told a complete stranger any such thing. A long, impatient wait in a grocery line is the least of our problems at any age, but the newness of feeling old, followed slowly but surely by a whole lot of other things that have never happened before, including that longing to quietly sit in a state of calm, felt worthy of comment to someone.

It wasn't easy at first to say, *I'm old*, or the slightly less scary, *I'm getting old*, to anyone, not even to myself. Like most people, I valued the opposite of old. We're told that changes in energy, appetite (including sexual appetite), strength, and our overall sense of well-being come with old age. An ache here, a creak there, an inexplicable weariness, and even the deep yearning to go into the blank —were these things, I'd ask myself, really about *old*? But then again, given I was in good health otherwise, it seemed obvious what they signaled. One day I understood in a bolt that the desire for a state of calm was exactly why the rocking chair was invented—probably by an older adult. When had I ever even thought about the comfort of a rocking chair before? Not ever.

Confusion, a longing to accept where I happened to be in life, frustration with new physical limitations, and the cultural denial that old age could possibly be a good thing all flooded into my mind. The turmoil usually led me only as far as the realm of stoicism, handed down from generations before me: *Get a grip. Bear up and be quiet. Nobody wants to hear about it.* Members of the Greatest Generation, as my parents' generation has been called, seemed comfortable with this approach. They'd lived through the Depression and a major war and were grateful for what they had. No crying or complaining allowed when old age came along. Their own parents and grandparents had either lived through a world war and a flu pandemic or succumbed to those things or something else for which there was no known cure at the time.

This daily, ordinary life brand of stoicism goes hand in hand with the predominant American culture and the era that I and millions of others grew up in. It figured strongly in midwestern American life. Nobody questioned it. *Life is hard and the work must get done.* If you didn't do the work, you would either die or you'd need to go somewhere else to live. Be quiet and don't complain were unwritten commands that came not only from the fields or nine-to-five jobs but from all directions: home, school, church, even the playground, where children had absorbed unquestioning endurance so completely they'd use it as a weapon if anyone showed an inkling of wanting to step back: Don't be a crybaby! Quitter! Loser!

If we're reasonably healthy, pretending that nothing much is happening to us may seem to serve us, at least for a while. This stance is fairly common for people with either extremely good luck or access to good medical care all their lives, or both. It's those other people in our age range who are old, the thinking goes, the ones compromised in some way. This kind of denial allows for saying things like, "I don't like being around old people," or, "I don't feel old," as if saying these things means the speaker is not old. It's not hard to feel compassion for this approach. After all, we can see what's coming for them if their lives continue on and on. All of us can pretend anything we want to, if we want to, until a day comes that forces us to join those other people in their vulnerability. As Jean Rhys writes, "At last you realize you'll never feel perfectly well again, never be able to move easily or see well or hear well, as the case may be."

As the case may be. The more I read about old age, the clearer it became that we've been taught to see "the old" as a single clump of people. That view makes us blind to the truth, which is that we each experience this time of life in a different way. Like our own growth from childhood into youth, like the aging we've done ever since, day by day, this span of life, too, is unique to each one of us.

Because it is personal, I'd assumed friends would greet my comments about aging that way, as in "Oh, so this is how it's going with you." Some did, especially those who were years older than I, but others continued to deny the experience, gently and kindly but firmly, and they were so sweet about it that it felt hard to insist facts were facts. We were all growing old.

The very old know that when old age enters us it's not about to turn around and leave. "For to think you're young when you're old is an impossibility," Jean Rhys writes in *My Day*. Its cover bears a photograph of the author that proves she is qualified to speak on the subject. White-haired, she sits against a dark background, head turned slightly away from the camera. Her large eyes, which have seen too awfully much of how women are treated—poor and dependent women, even beautiful and highly gifted women like her—now look with solemn curiosity toward something in the distance. "Old people are constantly reminded, every day," she writes, "every hour, almost every minute that they are old; only a lunatic wouldn't be convinced."

"No matter what," I say to myself and to my older friends, "this aging business is going to have its way with me." I say it to clear the air. I say it while knowing it's as obvious to all of us as that cover photograph of the white-haired Jean Rhys is to me—she who is often presented in any writing about her as her young and gorgeous self, ludicrous given that she wrote her most vivid and widely read novel starting in her fifties and working on it off and on until she published it in her seventies. To borrow her words, only a lunatic wouldn't be convinced that age brought also, in her case, mastery.

Yet yet yet . . . *How can I be old*, I'd ask myself in the quiet of my own mind back in those days of being a younger old person. Even now, years after that first hit of understanding what was happening, I sometimes ask myself the same thing. I ask it even though my logical answer is always, *Of course I'm old; I was born a long time ago.* I ask it anyway, knowing I would have had to be in complete denial not to expect it, what with day following day and year following year and all that. Yet it is quite something when it happens to you. Surprise! You, too, are a natural thing alive in a natural world that is ruled by—guess what—Nature.

One day in South Dakota, the winter sky stone gray, the air frigid, I got my first period. I'd had one or two false alarms the previous summer, but now finally here was the real deal: blood that kept on coming. I was fourteen.

My father, who worked at a department store, must have received a call about it from my mother because that night when he came home from work he brought me a gift, a new coat. It happened to be a red coat. I have no idea if he was tuned into the symbolism of that or not, but I doubt it. We were not a family that recognized or discussed symbols. In any case, this soft, wool, double-breasted, satin-lined garment wrapped around me in a heavenly way and fell all the way to my knees. Not a jacket. No. A full-length, grown-up lady coat.

We ate our dinner not speaking once of menstrual blood. I finished washing the dishes and started up to my room to do homework. When I reached the landing, I caught a glimpse of my parents out of the corner of my eye. They'd followed me to the living room and stood near the bottom of the stairs. They gazed up at me as if I'd become some wondrous creature alight on their very own staircase, willing to fall asleep on a bed in their very own house.

I felt magical without having done anything other than go along with life until this particular day happened. I turned slightly to look down at them as a princess might look down from her balcony at her subjects, and I smiled a beneficent princess smile at their awed and beaming faces. Then I ascended the rest of the way to my room, my books, my same life but to be lived now as someone *older*.

All of this happened without any of the three of us once mentioning the word "period," but my friends heard that word from me soon after, just as I'd heard it from them. I joined the club of menstruating girls and became privy to the code about visits from Aunt Flo, complaints about cramps, the borrowing and loaning of coins for the Kotex machine in the bathrooms at school, the giggles about near disasters and the shameful embarrassment when real disasters happened. We were adolescents together and that was that. Our periods, though they could be painful, opened up all kinds of possibilities, of course—reproduction for one, though we never mentioned that because, in a country with no access to legal abortion, we feared it. The main thing was that we were no longer children, a point registered, accepted, owned.

I want to speak to friends—or to anyone—about being old now with ease. I want the reality of what it feels like to be in this part of life to be heard and validated, not dwelled on necessarily but understood as a natural evolution of human life itself, undeniable. Truth matters as much here as anywhere else. I know a first period means a whole life lies waiting ahead and old age equals not so much time left, but I also know that I don't want youth again. If, like Jean Rhys, you are fortunate enough not to find yourself in a debilitating state of mind or body that calls on all your strength to survive or attend to, then these years of life, even with their grunts and growls of impatience, are, it turns out, plenty interesting. Even with difficulties, this time is profound in ways that are worth being present for and asking others to bear witness to.

I wince when I hear people apologize after only a sentence or two about what it feels like to be entering and passing through this quite natural span of life. Even if they do talk to their families or their best friends about aches and pains, when someone outside of those intimate relationships asks them how they are and they mention an ache, a disappointment in being now unable to do something, or real pain, they immediately look a little sheepish and say something like, "Sorry for the organ recital. I guess I'm not young anymore! Can't complain. Shouldn't complain. Don't mean to complain. Here I am, complaining! Lucky to be here at all!"

Should we say nothing in friendly company when a hip hurts because it's bone scraping bone in there? Is that a small matter unworthy of comment, *bone scraping bone?* Or maybe a usually reliable springboard of energy gives out in the middle of the morning, and it's unsettling to find yourself back in bed. Should we not mention how strange it is to find ourselves *back in bed at ten a.m.?* Or eyes are so dry they won't stop burning and it's hard to read and you love to read. You love to read, damn it. And here are the eyes doing this thing and eye drops aren't helping much. Or you can't drive at night anymore because your vision is failing, but you want to see your friends at night. You love your friends! You rely on them and they on you and they're slipping out of your reach. Or you fear death itself, which seems like it could happen at any moment now and you never thought about it quite that way before.

Addressing such things in serious conversation, especially one in which a younger person might be talking about her own body and its upsets and betrayals, or her own fears, should not call for any sort of apology. *She's* not apologizing. We didn't apologize to each other when we talked about how our bodies were changing in other ways, giving us those menstrual cramps or PMS, for example. Cramps are usually a lot less painful than arthritis, which does not limit itself to a few days a month.

Back in our youth, within each of us a uterus made itself known, and sometimes it hurt. As young and middle aged-women, we continued to talk to each other about our lives, including not only cramps but breast size, sexual orientation, childbirth, vaginal health, nursing, weight, miscarriages, abortions, D&Cs, assorted aches and pains, surgeries; even menopause finally made it to the table among women who barely knew one another at all. I once talked to a woman in an airport bathroom for ten minutes about what we were both going through with menopause. I never saw her again. It didn't matter. For us, the subject was wide open. Now we've added gender, transgender, cisgender. Women talking to women about these things is acceptable until our bodies start to make changes related to aging.

If we back away from talking freely about the challenges because they are unwelcome subjects or seem like "complaining," it's hard to talk freely about the *good* things that come with old age. Bodies continually change, that's the truth of the matter. Pretending a body's life is only worth discussing up to a point isn't honest. Taboos passed down from generation to generation against frank discussions of what aging feels like still exist; the denial of old age as a natural state still exists. Even so, we can commit to removing the barriers and shifting the conversation about what happens to us from being about "complaining" to being about sharing what growing older is for us.

Like their creator, the women in Jean Rhys's novels could be obsessed with their looks and with clothes. In *Voyage in the Dark*, for example, young Anna Morgan says, "All right, I'll do anything for good clothes. Anything—anything for clothes." So maybe it's no accident that the title essay of *My Day* was originally published in *Vogue*. In a poignant and sometimes funny way, this piece describes a typical day in the life of the author as experienced in her mid-eighties.

One of my favorite parts is the beginning, when she wakes before dawn in her darkened and wind-rattled house, mildly curious about the occasional *thunks* and moans she hears from its recesses. She realizes hours remain before her scheduled time to get up, so now she must decide whether to get up anyway, which will make her feel sleepy all day, or pick up a book from the few she keeps close to her bed and hope to fall back to sleep.

One of her nearby books is titled *Lo!* and it's "full of marvels and wonders," but she could also choose a murder mystery or a cookbook by Marcel Boulestin, in French. This last book is a long-time friend and Boulestin's lists of ingredients and authoritative instructions lull her. The cookbook also comforts her because it's designed in a way reminiscent of the nineteenth century, the century of her birth in Dominica. "The feeling of the book, the touch of it is reassuring," she writes. "I don't think of the nineteenth century as shut in, prejudiced. To me the nineteenth century is a large mango tree, orchids, sun, heaven, hell—which you could avoid—sudden darkness, huge stars."

Eventually she leaves both book and bed and rises to experience her day, drinking tea and on to reading the mail, avoiding unwelcome visitors from one of the many "ardent sects" around Devon, shopping with her devoted and amusing driver, and so on until night returns and she bolts the door of her rickety house.

Is my own day so very different? My houseboat doesn't rattle, but it gently rocks and sometimes sighs when a barge passes by. My bedside table also contains favorite books for when I wake up in the middle of the night, *Wide Sargasso Sea* and *My Day* among them. The simplicity of Jean Rhys's shopping trip is not so different from mine, though I'm able to do my own driving. She laments the changes made in the name of progress to a once pretty city, as I do. She takes careful note of certain interesting people when she's out and about, and so do I. She thinks of quotes from authors she likes. On the particular day she describes, she quotes Stevie Smith: "It's all very well to talk about the beauty of the human body, but I can think of a whole lot of other things more beautiful." So can Rhys, and she does: "Lions, cats, horses. What about hummingbirds, butterflies, even goldfish. Endless."

That became a favorite passage for me, but I find many quotes to guide me along or make me laugh, many of them from my mother or one of her many sisters. "I can either go somewhere or get ready to go somewhere," my Aunt Mattie used to say in her own old age. "I can't possibly do both." I think of that statement whenever I try to pack a suitcase.

Rhys finds herself more prone in her old age to pay attention to nature. This pleasure came to me fairly late in life, too. She feels a little fear sometimes at night, as many old and vulnerable people do, particularly women. The last essay of the book is titled "Close Season for the Old?" In it, she writes about the disappearance of a neighbor into a nursing home, the ways in which desire for independence can coexist with a need for help, the intolerable way the old are treated as if all the same, while each person is an individual, unique. She asks the question anyone who is old and thoughtful also asks: "Why not allow the old, whenever possible, to follow their bent without interference, malice or ridicule? Why must everyone be forced into this legendary uncomfortable bed—the right size for all—for which the tall have had their limbs lopped off and short have been racked and stretched to fit? The tiresome old will soon be quiet enough." She celebrates the surprising compensations: living in the present (what an enormous gift, I think as I read her assert it again), happiness for a day when one feels well or almost well, pleasure in small things (countless bursts of joy—countless!), the relief of events and certain relationships not mattering to that intense degree they used to matter (thank goodness). Calmness. This last is my *blank*, my precious and desired blank, that settling down within, though these days I'm more likely to find that calm in drawing and photography than staring out the window.

What Rhys doesn't discuss in these essays are her own losses. I wish she had. We gain great benefit from sharing what the many losses at this time of life feel like, of course, but also—if we allow ourselves to talk of them without apology, without throwing up a wall when we feel uncomfortable and declaring "that's enough of that," if we go on as freely as we like—maybe we can make the whole of life more real to younger people so that they're not quite as blindsided as we were—at least as much as my generation seems to be—with the arrival of old age.

Why not give voice to the all of it when the all of it includes loss? I welcome it when someone shares the loss of a beloved friend or partner of thirty-three, forty-two, sixty-five years dies, or a dearest, sweetest companion, an aged dog or cat, a mother or father, an old neighbor that they loved to see and chat with regularly, a sister that they talked to every single night on the phone. There's a heap of bereavement that comes along. Over dinner one evening, Celia, my mother's closest friend in the assisted living facility where both lived, said, "Doesn't it all make you want to scream sometimes?" My mother agreed and later told me about this exchange and how she appreciated the honesty of it.

Up until then, I had not understood how all that piling on of loss might make you want to scream sometimes. Most people I knew at the time and mentioned it to, including those who read my blog about my mother in her nineties, didn't seem aware of that feeling. Why doesn't everyone know and discuss the fact that of course this must be how it might be for many, at least now and then? It's not mentioned or even guessed at, yet here sat two old women in a room of at least fifty others, many of whom, I could suddenly and clearly see, had probably felt exactly the same way. The old are perceived as trouble if they complain, perceived as trouble if they're encumbered by any disability or serious illness, perceived as trouble if they need too much care. Imagine if it became common knowledge that, along with these things, with some, at times, there's an urge to scream. Many wouldn't like hearing this unpleasant fact, but for many others—perhaps a significantly larger number—it would strip away the sugar coating of "sweet old lady" and allow for taking in that growing older can be complex and difficult at times.

Even while deeper realities may be unknown or ignored, the old get credit for being great resources for stories of bygone days. I can almost always tell who's open to listening to the truth about my life versus those who only want to hear a story about my long-gone youth. I like telling those stories; they're fun to relive. But youth is not the only time that's interesting. We don't need to talk about every "jerk," as Jean Rhys called the changes that bring us into old age, but we also don't need to stay silent because others might fidget and squirm a little when hearing what it's like to be standing on this stage of life.

For me, the inside of old means the familiar, lived-in self is saying new things. Saying: *Stop now and rest.* Saying: *Would it feel good in the long run to do that or will it cause pain later?* Saying: *Didn't I lose my keys last week too? Uh-oh. Should I worry?* Saying: *I like being old sometimes, this perspective on things.* Saying: *Yes, I talk to my dead, and sometimes I think I hear them talking back to me, and so what?* Saying: *Look at all the aliveness I feel this morning, right this moment; I should do something fun with it.* Saying: *What an amazing thing it is to know what I need when I need it. I wonder why that used to be so hard.* Saying: *Whoa! What is this sudden sharp pain in my middle finger? Am I suppressing an obscene gesture toward someone in the news or should I google "sharp pain in middle finger?" If I do the last thing, am I actually going to follow up with the doctor or try to forget about it and hope it never happens again?* Saying: *Old age is a privilege. The full span: a miracle.* Saying: *I want to scream sometimes.* Saying: *I like myself and other people better than I ever have.*

Some of what's shared will be hard to hear. There can be pain. That is truth. But pain can come at any age. There's more to it than that. There is the poetic, the inspirational, the fact of worlds within this world of old, amazing to experience. Old age is layered and complex, not a place we arrive, like the dentist's office. It lasts a long time, with plenty to say and feel and do and not do. I hope new arrivals to these years don't persist in the silence of our predecessors, so many of whom were abandoned in the "dentist's office" for thirty or forty years. I hope we can say all we need and want to say right out loud and toss any unconsciously agreed upon stoicism to the wind. I believe it's possible, even likely, for us to contribute by being a much more vocal bunch than our parents and grandparents. We deserve to be seen and heard, just as they did.

At the library bookstore many years ago, I found the authentic voice of a woman willing to speak her experience. It's from her, Jean Rhys, that I got the idea that it's a gift to bear witness to this time of life. Long after finding that book, I discovered that the "My Day" essay is also included at the end of her autobiography, *Smile Please*. Even so, I like to read it in the small volume I found years ago. Whenever I pick it up, it reassures me, just as the hefty French cookbook she kept by her bedside reassured her. In *My Day*, she told the truth. She could not turn around and again be her beautiful young self writing in Paris or playing with her childhood friends back in the West Indies. She could only be who she was at the time, an old woman, like those of us who are now old women with all that entails: orchids, sun, heaven, hell, sudden darkness, huge stars.

The Old Woman in Time

In summer, I like to read and eat meals on my houseboat's upper deck. Throughout the day, I watch the river's color shift from silver in the morning to the glossy blue-green of high noon, changing to emerald green and gold as the day ages. Eventually it arrives at its lavender close. I look out at raptors, songbirds, turtles, otters, beavers—whatever comes my way. One June day I decided to take a book just received in the mail, *A History of Old Age*, outside with me. I'd sent for it as a gift to myself.

Published by the J. Paul Getty Museum, *A History of Old Age* is a collection of essays with examples of works of art. I'd been wanting a wider view, a historic view. That spring I'd been reading novels by writers of previous generations, windows into the lives of older women in their day: Doris Lessing's *The Diary of a Good Neighbor*; Leonora Carrington's *The Hearing Trumpet*; Elizabeth Taylor's *Mrs. Palfrey at the Claremont*; *Quartet in Autumn* by Barbara Pym. Reading novels like these drove home the fact that all the women who lived beyond fifty or sixty in all the generations that preceded me had to face this monumental change and find a way to deal with it in their own way, as I do. I always feel hungry for more about these lives, but if it's challenging to find contemporary novels with older women at the center of a story, it's even harder as you go into the past. Also, many of the portraits that do exist in literature before the twentieth century were written by men, often younger men.

How else to find her then, the old woman in time? I'd spent quite a few hours poring over photographs from the nineteenth century. Occasionally I spotted someone at work on a farm or captured by the camera on the street or as she stood among family members in a casual way, but mostly I found both older men and women sitting stiffly posed like everyone else regardless of age, their images taken from a distance. The more of these images I saw, the more curious I became about portrayals in previous centuries. How did an older woman go about her daily life? How did others see her? How did she see herself? Photography couldn't take me there. To see these women of earlier times close up and witness how they fared and try to imagine my way into their lives, it became clear I'd need to turn to other art. *A History of Old Age*, even with its limited, primarily European scope, came into grateful hands.

From my perch above the river, I opened the large book of glossy pages and began to look into the eyes of those who'd lived into old age long before me. While many of these works were, like the photographs, posed portraits, there were also plenty of people engaged in the fluidity of life. Although these subjects left no texts behind, I could witness their interests, their work, their place and meaning within their families and societies.

A History of Old Age covers Greek and Roman times through the end of the twentieth century. Though it includes some American works, its European focus leaves out women across the planet and over centuries of time, but at least it gave me a place to begin. I would see faces that resembled my ancestors. Nearby, in a nest under the eaves that had been used by their ancestors for generations, I could hear swallow fledglings daring each other to fly at least as far as the deck's railing. With these half-fearful, half-joyful cries and the shifting light on the river as my companions, I dove in.

It wasn't the art in the book that made me understand what the poets see when observing nature and light and the parallels to human life. That happens to all of us, if not through our own observation then not long after our reading lives begin. By the time we come across Shakespeare's Sonnet 73, it's spelled out for us:

> That time of year thou mayst in me behold
> When yellow leaves, or none, or few, do hang
> Upon those boughs which shake against the cold,
> Bare ruin'd choirs, where late the birds sang.

If we still don't get it on our own, teachers point it out (although not one of my teachers ever mentioned that some scholars believe this sonnet may have been written lovingly to a younger man). Many of these works of art brought a different poetry, a way to witness both the travails and beauty of aging, and the way the light fades differently on different faces. As I leafed through the pages, I began to feel my way into where I stand as yet another old woman in time and in relation to nature and light, as I live now, on the cusp of the lavender closing. I found faces somewhat similar in texture and lines to my own and could stare at them in a way I can't quite stare into the faces of my friends or would even have attempted to do with my mother when she reached her seventies, the time when I'd first noticed old age taking a firmer hold.

Although wrinkles and crow's feet are the most commonly acknowledged facial signatures of a woman aging, there's so much more to see in old faces. For example, the eyelids drop and the eyes themselves appear to recede into the skull; pores enlarge; spots rise to the surface from some inner well of light brown hue and scatter the cheeks, chin, and forehead with abandon, a sort of Jackson Pollock effect; tiny pearly cysts poke like pinheads through cheeks; hair withdraws from eyelashes, temples, and eyebrows and migrates to the nose, where it flourishes; gum lines recede; whiskers gather in little crowds on the chin; the nose leaps forward. In the paintings of centuries past, many of these things appear, created by masters and in full color. Almost all of the subjects of these paintings looked beautiful to me. Whether they looked that way to themselves at the time, I couldn't know. I especially loved the kindly face of *Old Woman with Green Scarf* by Christian Seybold (1794) and *The Lacemaker* by Bernhard Kiel (1660), a face lit with character and grace. I found myself wishing to talk to these two women.

All that summer, when I climbed to my perch to check on the progress of the puffs of feathers busy testing out the sturdiness of the railing, a few more pages would absorb me for an hour or so. It was slow going because I'd pause now and then to read selections from essays that described conditions for the old in each era covered. Generalizations may abound, but diversity and variety are clear in the ways people live and have always lived through a stretch of time that can be as long as thirty or forty—even fifty— years. As Pat Thane writes in the first chapter: "'Old people' include some of the fittest and some of the most decrepit, some of the richest and some of the most powerful and the poorest and most marginalized people in any society."

I'd always believed the old had only recently fallen from grace. In some previous time, so I'd heard, they would have expected respect and care. I'd held on to my belief through the years, but several paintings and some of the essays in *A History of Old Age* pricked that balloon. Georges de La Tour's *Couple Eating Peas*

(1618), for example, is a portrait of a man and woman in their sixties, or possibly fifties, who are digging hungrily into small bowls
of peas. Malnourishment meant it was common among the poor
to lose teeth, vibrancy, and vigor; in other words, to live as if quite
old even if they weren't. Through La Tour's painting and others
like it, I quickly learned that at least European societies didn't feel
any sort of calling to take care of the nutritional needs of older
adults who lived either in poverty or close to it.

Some elders were honored, especially if they owned property
and controlled an extended family's purse strings, but the paintings showed others shuttled off to poor houses or begging on the
streets. A few social safety nets existed here and there, but, according to the book's text, most of these, such as hospitals, were limited in terms of the numbers of the aged they could take in. This
meant that a large number of people lived under the pressure to
work until they literally dropped. Meanwhile, as they neglected
the very people whose labor each new generation stood on, it was
apparent from the art that European communities enjoyed seeing
their elders as objects of derision. Only that single condition of
wealth more or less reliably offered an alternative. Of course the
majority of older adults had none.

It didn't surprise me that artists chose to show the harshness of
the plight of the old through time, especially their poverty. Who
better to have sympathy? What I didn't understand until finding
A History of Old Age was that some artists lacked a humane spirit
and would not only poke fun of their subjects but denigrate them
in other ways, depicting them as hideous and frightening—particularly old women. Peter Brueghel the Elder, he of the crowded
village scenes, painted a peasant woman in a way that seems intended to rouse scorn and laughter. Hans Baldung Grien, a student of Dürer, did something similar with another woman of mea-
ger means. Was he chuckling, I wondered (this man proves to be

the most sexist artist in these pages), as he exposed one shrunken breast, implying that even in her wretched ugliness, at least as he sees her, she's still trying to earn money as a prostitute? This piece, *Study of an Old Woman*, is more commonly known as either *The Witch* or *The Hag*. Born in the fifteenth century, this artist was one of the first to create images that became known as the witch. Using his considerable skill, he gave an accepted form to crude and cruel beliefs. He could turn any old woman into an ugly and malevolent creature, presenting her in a way that suggested evil powers. This supposedly supercharged being could control fate, instigate wickedness, bring harm, even fly. Although he painted portraits and other subjects, Hans Baldung Grien stuck with the theme of "the witch" and her dark influence throughout his life.

The more esteemed an artist was, the more he could amplify disrespect, whether that was his intention or not. My heart sank as I came to believe that, in some cases, that was exactly the intention. Post-menopausal women were believed by many to be filled with ill humors triggered by the end of menstruation. These toxins supposedly backed up into their systems, poisoning their minds. Ever since Eve, women had been troublesome. Let them reach old age and they're double trouble. The poorest of women were the worst because their diets were filled with unhealthy and often indigestible food. Their bodies responded with distress and so the effects of poor diet made them even more likely to be seen as "poisoned" or, in other words, problematic.

Whenever I turned a page and another woman's face appeared on a canvas painted hundreds of years ago, I thought about what might have been *her* story of her aging body. How had she reacted when she realized that her own precious life intersected with ways older adults were seen and treated? Did she wonder if these behaviors would change in her time? In the future? Servant, mistress, worker, wife, rich or poor, each of these subjects once held opinions about growing old herself and the old in general, as all humans do. Each one had lived her middle age right up until she could no longer deny she was old, at least as far as those around her saw it. Some of these women must have felt puzzled about the discrepancy between their knowledge that they were the same people they'd always been and perceptions of them as they aged, which ranged from veneration to amusement to irritation to the infliction of true misery, based on their appearance.

I became curious about how these subjects felt about the works of art resulting from sitting patiently in certain clothes and in certain lighting to be drawn or painted. Did they later feel regret? Facing some of these paintings, they wouldn't be looking at their true selves, which contained all of their ages, but a male painter's view of them—as women no longer fertile or beautiful, and therefore worth little, even laughable.

Had an old woman actually posed for Francisco Goya's etching, *Linda Maestra*, known in English as *A Fine Teacher* or *Pretty Teacher*? This is one of the pieces in his series called *Los Caprichos (The Caprices)*. An early advertisement for the sale of *Los Caprichos* prints in 1799 provides a description that maybe Goya had written himself, stating that the artist has chosen subjects "among the multitude of extravagances and follies which are common throughout civilized society. . . ." Although the series offers both aristocracy and clergy as viable subjects for ridicule, the advertisement describes the pieces as whimsical and states that the artist used only his imagination, not any specific people as models. He placed these works for sale in a perfume and liquor store near his apartment. According to the advertisement, the pieces were meant for the artist to explore "vulgar prejudices and frauds rooted in custom, ignorance or interest."

I felt relieved that no woman had been used as a model for the nightmarish scene. In the etching, two women, one young and the other much older, ride a broomstick into the night sky. For Goya, born almost three hundred years after Baldung Grien, the witch-on-a-broomstick-in-flight image was common. The woman nearer to the top of this particular broomstick, the driver so to speak, is bent, gaunt, and slightly smiling; the other woman, her body young, full, and lush, holds onto her. This work contains an owl hovering above. I searched for more information and learned this was a common symbol in Spain at the time for prostitute. Because of this owl, many would see the old woman as a procuress. The caption in *A History of Old Age* doesn't mention this, but it does describe the old woman as someone meant to be perceived as "dangerous" and explains that this is "a curious belief founded partly on mistaken medieval ideas, partly on the guilty knowledge that they generally had a just grievance against society."

Fearing the danger of "just grievance" could easily be one of the reasons men's eyes dart away when they see us coming. Treat girls and women badly throughout their whole lives and even the average Joe can figure out why a crone might like to give him a swat, or worse.

The "mistaken medieval ideas" mentioned translated to torture and death for many. When Goya created this piece, Europe had spent the past couple of hundred years on witch hunts, trying to rid itself of those they deemed treacherous by mutilating and killing them. There's no agreement on how many people died during this insanity, but some historians estimate around twelve thousand in mainland Europe alone, with more dying in England and Scotland, as well as the American colonies.

Estimates are that around 80 percent of these so-called witches were women, many advanced in years and poor, accused of witchcraft not only for all those juices backing up inside and poisoning them (hard to prove, even in a prejudicial court), but for planting a garden with herbs to address ills and aches, or working as a midwife to alleviate the pain of childbirth, thereby scorning God, who said to Eve, "I will greatly increase your pains in childbearing; with pain you will give birth to children" (Genesis 3:16). The widowed, the demented, the gifted, the women perceived as burdens by their families—all lived in danger of hanging or death by fire.

I couldn't look at Goya's witch on her broomstick more than two hundred years later and pretend what happened to those women no longer mattered, whether he was exposing superstition or creating more of it himself. I recognized what I'd already seen of Goya's work was masterful. He'd influenced Manet, Dali, Picasso, and many others, and he refused sentiment and mannerism. Of course it was likely he was satirizing the brutally cruel beliefs that inspired witch hunts. Yet, as an old woman of today, I felt perturbed by that little smile on the older woman's face and the possibility of a male smirk behind the given title, *Pretty Teacher*.

In her caption, Pat Thane asserts this etching underscores the myth of the dangerous old woman. The younger woman isn't forced to climb aboard and hang on. She does it willingly. Such an image would arouse fear in the hearts of men who considered themselves good. An aged female teaching sexual knowledge and occult crafts, or even speaking negatively about the patriarchy as the two ride naked together through the night on a symbolic phallus that they control, is a threat. A young woman would definitely not learn goodness in that situation. It's even possible, God forbid, she'd learn the meaning of *just grievance* in a world without justice for women.

As I looked at *Pretty Teacher*, I found myself imagining a late afternoon in Madrid in 1799. An old woman walks slowly toward home, passing closed shops along a street that happened to be called Calle del Desengaño, Disappointment Street. Her arms and shoulders ache from a long day hunched over heavy fabrics she sews together for an upholsterer, but she's grateful for work at her age. Her eyes long for something pleasant to see, so she stops to peer into the perfume shop window. A sign out front names one of her neighbors, the well-known artist who lives nearby. She spots *Pretty Teacher* and tries to take in what she sees: a figure around her own age with a back curved like a frog, hair receding and wild as seaweed, shriveled bottom seated on a broom ascending into the night. *Witch. Procuress. Teacher of terrible things.* Even if she understands the famous artist in the neighborhood is commenting on how lack of reason can run insanely amok, she nevertheless might think, "You're not doing us old women any favors here, Francisco."

I pursued more of Goya's nightmare images of the old, their wasted bodies and grim pursuits, including devouring babies. An entire collection, I learned, had been on display in Goya's *Witches and Old Women* exhibit at the Courtauld Gallery in London in 2015. The gallery's posting about the work explains that Goya originally intended it for only a few people in his life and goes on to discuss the range of his imagination, evident in work showing superstition, nightmares, and the "problems of old age." The description ends this way: "Above all, the drawings reveal Goya's penetrating observation of human nature: our fears, weaknesses, and desires."

It's hard to look at these portrayals of brutality, malice, and sickening predilections as associated with mature human beings. The gorging on babies is particularly chilling, especially when one older woman does it while looking boldly and directly at the viewer with cold eyes. I wondered who the Courtauld meant by "our" in "our fears, weaknesses and desires." Since this statement includes contemporary viewers as well as those from the era of superstition in which the work was done, does this mean we're supposed to be finding ourselves "penetratingly observed?"

In his *New York Times* review of the Titian exhibit at the Isabella Stewart Gardner Museum—*Women, Myth and Power* (2021), which includes *The Rape of Europa*—critic Holland Cotter explains we are now in an age when we can no longer look at art and experience it as exempt from moral scrutiny. He writes that, in order to find appreciative new audiences for older art, facts about it have to be addressed so that it can be seen both "as formally superlative creations, but also as container of difficult, often negative histories." (*New York Times*, August 12, 2021, "Can We Ever Look at Titian's Paintings the Same Way Again?")

Even if the collected works in *Witches and Old Women* had been intended only to express Goya's own nightmares or as satire, images of old as nightmare, as demonic, demented, decayed, destructive, debilitated, deplorable, and undesirable were scattered over the centuries before him, with aging itself presented as a dreadful state and some of the cruelest representations reserved for women. One of the earliest of such depictions, *The Ugly Duchess* (1513) by Quentin Matsys (no Prince Charming himself), could have set the tone for the old woman as fair game for mockery and disgust. The portrait may have been based on a woman sick with a disfiguring disease called Paget's, but it was accepted for centuries as satire, not a depiction of illness. The older woman has a shrunken appearance. She wears a dress that features her breasts, in the fashion of her youth, and she holds a red flower, which symbolizes her desire for passion. Some think it sprang from Matsys's reading of the famous essay by Erasmus called "In Praise of Folly," in which old women wanting to be admired "still play the coquette . . . and do not hesitate to show their repulsive withered breasts."

I raised my head and inhaled the fresh air of forest and river, took in the happy chirrups and short flights of the young swallows. Dealing in the dark arts, moldering in their own skins, jaunting around on broomsticks, eating babies, wearing silly clothes, luring customers into a brothel with the flash of a fallen and flattened breast—talk about a witchy brew. "Dear Sisters in Old Age," I might write in a letter to send back through time, "with 'fine' artists like these, who needs enemies?"

But I knew that before any portrayals of old women on canvas came to be, the ideas behind them had been stirred for a long time in multiple thousands of conversations stemming from cultural, mythological, and religious beliefs. All of that had anchored ageism and misogyny in the collective European mind where it could be passed on from one generation to the next without question. I realized that of course artists, too, encoded and passed these negative messages on.

In most of the paintings in *A History of Old Age*, men look generally more prosperous, healthy, and attractive than a lot of the women. It's understandable because the majority of them had access to more money and standing. But also, most of these artists knew how to see their fellows. Very few could have looked at a woman, let alone an old woman, in an unprejudiced way because of their inherited ideas about them and the skewed artistic versions of them already in existence.

Nevertheless, the paintings offered a chance to see the many differences among the old that Pat Thane mentioned early in the book. They showed a wide range of physical abilities, clothing, tasks, cozy homes or poor shelter. I grew attached to a few of the faces in the portraits and scenes, and over the summer I returned often to them. I especially liked two seventeenth-century portraits, probably of the same woman, by Pietro Belotti. One is titled *Atropos* and the other simply *An Old Woman*. Her creased face and frank gaze drew me right in. I could easily imagine a complex and interesting life for the woman who sat for these.

I also grew fond of the careworn face of another lace maker. She sits in a dark room, at work. The portrait was painted in 1655 by Nicholas Maes. Making lace, I learned, was one of the things older women could continue to do in order to earn a bit of money so they could put off going to a poorhouse or into the streets to beg. I compared the worn face to the one belonging to the woman in "Portrait of an Old Lady" (1755) by Joachim Martin Kalbe, which does not show much wear at all. This wealthy crone sits serenely wrapped in silk and yards of lace. She'd probably been oblivious to the existence of her lace maker or those of any era. In her life of great privilege, she couldn't know what it would take for old eyes and old fingers to create this much adornment for a single dress. On one hand she wears a fine leather glove; the other is bare, pale, and smooth as a girl's. You can't look at those hands and imagine that either of them had ever lifted itself on behalf of another person. But I still appreciated the way her wide open eyes seem to be saying to the artist, "So you're going to study me closely, are you? Well, keep in mind I'm also looking closely at you, and maybe I see more about you than you can possibly see about me."

Only a couple of women artists appear in the book. One of them is Sofonisba Anguissola (1532–1625). Along with many other portraits and works, she painted self-portraits throughout her life. In the portrait of herself at the age of seventy-eight (1610), the Italian artist is seated. Is she thinking about her age, her death, her many accomplishments, all of these things? She's dressed beautifully—she was born to a noble family and was eventually a court artist in Spain. Maybe because of her status, her history of self-portraiture, her own nature and gifts, and the fact that, at a young age, her work had won the admiration of Michelangelo, she presents herself for view with confidence. Because European women weren't allowed to be trained as artists, to find one who was not only trained but masterful is rare, to see her in old age even rarer. Although this was her last self-portrait, she lived to be ninety-three.

Seated at tables or on stools, benches, and chairs and dressed in their rags, workaday clothing, Sunday best, or finery, none of the other women portrayed could do what Anguissola had done. They couldn't be artists, only subjects. How could they avoid feeling judged for their faces and bodies? No matter how free-thinking the artist, he still painted someone not considered in his time to be his equal: first, she was a woman; second, an old woman. You can't live a long life unaware of how men see you (or don't see you). If I feel instantly dismissed by a man's eyes in passing on the street, what must it have been like for any of these hunched and wrinkled women, even if wealthy, to sit before a male painter and surrender to his vision, filtered through his limited understanding of her, day after day, for many hours at a time?

I paged through the book several more times that summer. There was no paradise for the old revealed by any of those paintings, no magical cloak of respect and dignity bestowed on them when they reached a certain age, but whatever the artists' intentions, I kept finding beauty in these women and men. Along with paintings I found scattered throughout other collections, they offer a glimpse into the lives of the aged through time. I felt gratitude to the artists, who, despite any gender-determined restrictions or their motivations, made the invisible woman, the old woman, visible. Although nearly all the faces are white, the examples gave me a range of ages, abilities, employment, living situations, passions, pursuits, values, and destinies to think about. The old woman in time I went searching for had revealed herself to me, at least in part and through a very narrow lens, in *A History of Old Age*.

The book reminded me that the meaning of old can be found only by looking at the old themselves, not turning away. It can't be guessed at or conjured but must be seen (and also lived) in order to know what it offers and what it takes away. There are as many different ways to be old as there are people who have lived and are living through this time of life.

On one of the last pages of *A History of Old Age* is another self-portrait, this one by artist Alice Neel at eighty (1980). Neel is one of the few Americans represented. She painted many other women throughout her long life. One of her themes was to turn the idealistic Madonna/Child trope on its head as she pursued other dimensions in portraits of mothers with their children and pregnant women. Her approach to this subject allows for conflict, forbearance, and women's strength. When Hilton Als curated some of her work at the David Zwirner gallery in New York (2021), the art critic spoke of her honesty: "I love her because she doesn't cheapen human experience with sentiment."

In terms of being sentimentalized, old age can easily compete with motherhood. Saccharine images of the old are popular and easy to find. But in her self-portrait at eighty, Alice Neel stays true to her principles. She does not hold back in painting herself, ever the humanist, sugar-coating nothing. In the self-portrait she sits naked and leaning slightly forward in a blue and white striped chair holding a paintbrush and a cloth. It's a mesmerizing painting, to me anyway, because it shouts legitimacy. White-haired, shoulders stooped, breasts drooping, and belly protruding, she looks straight out at the viewer. The painting may strike repulsion, even fear, in some, but whatever inner hoops a person must jump through in order to fully see her, Neel refuses to help them out by hiding. Like Sofonisba Anguissola, she shows herself as she is—accomplished, honest, smart, fearless, old, and, most importantly, wholly *visible*.

Maybe Alice Neel found it easy to paint and reveal her physical self in this image—but somehow I doubt it. Maybe the mothers in her paintings found it easy to see themselves represented in all the complexity of trying to raise children, especially as some lived in poverty or near poverty, with or without partners to help them, struggling to care or caring so very much about those who were dependent on them. I doubt that, too. I imagine that it had to be hard for some of these women to see themselves painted so realistically. To model for any artist is to take a risk. But Neel's subjects were not being tricked into allowing a representation of something they were not and were never objects of ridicule. The paintings of mothers and pregnant women are devoid both of sentiment and revulsion. When I looked at the self-portrait in old age by Neel, I sensed her openness: *Here is what I see.* Pages earlier in the book, I'd felt some other minds closing: *Here is what I fear.* The subjects, in each case, are human beings.

When I finally put the book aside, I kept returning to the same question: How can we, the older adults of today, bring something new and badly needed into previously accepted but prejudicial perceptions around aging? Whatever we do could begin with making ourselves seen, but how do we do that when our society instructs us to look away, meaning that eventually so many of us will look away from our very selves? If the task is to be seen and known in order to be treated as real and complete human beings and not as a group to be cast aside and forgotten, then I'm hoping more people will step into that question of how. For me, wondering how to do that has been a driver for writing this book.

A History of Old Age left me with respect for the ancient ones who walked this earth long before us, along with sadness that there weren't many more Sofonisba Anguissolas, more Alice Neels. We need great quantities of truth told about being old until being old becomes fully allowed as the natural and desired outcome of a life. This is our time. We can speak our reality as it manifests in our lives. Who knows our truths, our feelings, our stories, our tangible, perceptible, definite, unique selves better than we do?

The Queen and I

Wrapped in black and purple velvet, the Evil Queen stands before the Magic Mirror in Walt Disney's *Snow White and the Seven Dwarfs*. The last time she came to this mirror, she learned Snow White had replaced her as fairest in the land. This time, she believes she'll get her position back because she has ordered her huntsman to kill her rival and bring her the girl's heart. Although she triumphantly holds a box with a decoration showing a sword plunged through a heart, the Magic Mirror does not oblige her. It announces that Snow White still lives.

I watched this scene after seeing an episode of *American Experience* on PBS that featured Walt Disney. The program contained a clip from the first mirror scene in *Snow White and the Seven Dwarfs*, and it made me curious. What happened next? I couldn't recall, but I did remember that when I'd watched this film as a child, all my sympathies were with Snow White. I thought the Queen should understand that this girl was the fairest; shame on her for feeling angry about it. But this time it was the dilemma of the Queen that spoke to me.

The majority of us are not and have never been "the fairest of all." In her book *Metropolitan Life*, Fran Liebowitz wrote, "All God's children are not beautiful. Most of God's children are, in fact, barely presentable." When I look in the mirror, I don't see either. If it's a good day, the mirror reflects back to me other facets and faces of my life: both of my grandmothers, my child self, my father, some of my mother, and a bit of both of my brothers and my sister, along with the road I've traveled, separate from any of these connections. I can draw some peace from looking at this familiar self, my companion through this lifetime and what others see as me. Other days, wobblier days is how I think of them, I look in the mirror and have a different experience. Right under my very eyes, bags are packing new bags. Where'd they come from? The flesh of my cheeks looks like it's trying to escape its long-term love affair with bone: *You don't own me. Let me go!*

I turn up the volume on a little reality talk. *Well, what am I supposed to do? The changes in my face and, for that matter, my neck are real. I tell myself I can't reverse gravity; no magical substance will push everything back into place.* But equally loud on the wobbly days is another voice, the one claiming something has gone *wrong* somehow. An old face and an old body don't count for much.

I was experiencing a wobbly day when the mirror scenes in *Snow White* struck a nerve. When I saw the Queen again, I recognized her as the part of me that's trapped in the mirror, the part that pops up now and then and tells me that old isn't a good look. Although I've never lived on the same high pedestal of beauty she's falling from, I, too, am facing the fact of being regarded differently than I used to be. Both the Queen and I are disappearing from view.

The first time I knew that I was vanishing happened in my early sixties. One day in the cafeteria of the building where I worked, a man around forty or so elbowed past me in line. I tapped him on the shoulder and said that I'd been waiting and he shouldn't cut the line. He said, "Oh, I didn't see you. I'm sorry."

His apology sounded sincere but baffling. He actually hadn't seen me? I was five eight, only about two inches shorter than he was; our overall size was not that much different either. Not long after that experience I started to notice that strangers who passed me on the streets of this friendly city, where I've lived since the 1970s, didn't look at me anymore, or, if they did look, they allowed only a glance before their eyes darted away.

The eye dart didn't only happen on the street. It happened at the library, the pharmacy, in the bookstore, the food co-op— all over town. So what that people had never been agog at the sight of me, it still felt odd that eyes so deliberately and so swiftly looked away. My clothing style hadn't changed for decades: jeans or slacks and a shirt of some kind or, in cold weather, a sweater. Hair combed. Face washed. Nothing altered on the inside. On the outside: definitely older. It felt like I'd blended into the urban landscape, another parking meter or telephone pole. In at least one way, this felt freeing. I was no longer in the line of the male gaze, that is, no longer being assessed by my appearance alone as being of some value or of no value at all. This freedom felt energizing. Meanwhile, I was becoming more and more fascinated with nearly every old person I saw on the street or anywhere else. I had to try not to stare. Who were they? What were their stories? What did they think about getting older?

Disney's Queen isn't a curious sort of person. She isn't all that old, either. She looks, at the most, maybe slightly past forty. (Released in 1938, *Snow White and the Seven Dwarfs* had six directors, all men; eight writers worked on the project, only one of them a woman, so forty apparently represented the limit for "youthful" beauty.) But the Queen interested me because she makes the uncomfortable feelings around disappearing hard to miss. She doesn't for one second try to behave herself and quietly slip into the background like a good little old lady would. She doesn't stop to ask herself what her own opinion about her own face is either. She skips right past any wonder about growing old and allows the mirror's judgment to push her straight into white hot fury. Anger overwhelms any other emotion that might be percolating around the fact she's no longer meeting the accepted cultural norm of what a woman ought to be, including that death itself is what an aging face signals. No wonder our own eyes sometimes look back at us from the mirror in a sad, helpless, and judging way: *Why did you let this getting old business happen? Did you forget what comes next?*

At least we don't think about killing anybody. In the Disney universe, and in the original fairy tale, too, the Queen believes she must take matters into her own hands. She must get rid of someone who looks better than she does.

I paused the video to indulge in a brief fantasy of what a therapist would tell her at this point. Wasn't she completely misreading her situation? Obviously, my imaginary therapist would say, Snow White isn't the problem; it's all about the passage of time, and that's out of your control. And there are some other things, too, that you should be thinking about. But there you go, heading down a path of destruction.

The Queen's rush in the wrong direction starts the very moment she gets the news she's no longer the fairest and the box she holds contains not a girl's heart but a pig's. Disney sends her racing down the castle stairs to the basement, hell bent on ending the rivalry all by herself (damn that soft-hearted huntsman).

In a dimly lit chamber, her tapered fingers fly over a set of books on a cobwebbed shelf—*Alchemy, Black Arts, Sorcery, Black Magic*—and land on a volume titled *Disguises*. Her movements in her velvet cloak and oddly tight, yet flattering, headgear are so flowing and beautiful, her eyebrows such a drama unto themselves, that it's almost hard not to root for her a little. *Disguises.* Isn't this exactly where so many women of a certain age turn? The disguises provided by hair dye, make-up, face-lifts, Botox, and teeth whitening, but not—I can probably safely say never—how to look like a peddler, which is the Queen's choice.

With devilishly long fingernails, she taps at the instructions. Mummy dust goes into a goblet first, followed by a few drops of night to provide cover for her velvet clothes. "To age my voice, an old hag's cackle," the Queen explains to a terrified crow, who flutters into and out of a nearby human skull. The cackle is boiled up in a flask and delivered into the goblet. "To whiten my hair, a scream of fright." For this, she turns a spigot that releases both a ghost and a cry of terror.

Transformed, she does not, in any way, resemble a trustworthy, or even an untrustworthy, peddler. She looks exactly like a witch as we all have come to expect a witch to look. She immediately consults her book of spells for how to put poison into an apple that will bring about Snow White's "sleeping death."

You can bet the King, and one does exist in this story, isn't in some other wing of the castle racing down to dungeon territory to mix up a potion that will destroy a younger, more handsome guy. A king may have his reasons to want to kill a prince, but they'd never be related to physical appearance, even in a fairy tale. Although the King has no speaking part and isn't even pictured in a gilded frame hanging on the wall, the misery of the Queen's predicament comes straight out of patriarchy, wherein a woman's looks and youth are the most prized things about her. Once she disappoints the mirror that passes judgment on her (in a male voice, no less), she's as good as dead, or at least with one foot in the void. Yet, even with stakes this high, she, or in fact any woman who works in an obviously desperate way to sidestep that void, is supposed to make us cringe. Her wrong turn toward attempted murder ensures we despise her. Something is wrong with *her*, not with the system she finds herself in.

As a little girl watching this, I was unaware of what's left out of the story. The Queen didn't cook up this harsh situation all by herself. Watching these scenes again reminded me that I'd only recently come across an 1800 French print (artist unknown) that shows two old women sitting before their mirrors with younger women helping them. One aids her mistress with a cap to cover her (probably sparse) hair; the other helps hers put on a contraption that will make it appear as if she still boasts a pair of firm breasts. The younger pair look as if they can barely stifle laughter as they meet the viewer's eyes. *We must indulge these vain crones hovering on the brink of death.* The two women looking at themselves in their mirrors were much older than Disney's Queen, but they lived within the same system, and, like her, they wanted nothing to do with what the passing of time was doing to them. We are meant to laugh at them and feel contempt for their futile attempts to regain the prize of youth. Pathetic! We're not supposed to ask why they're so frightened, what's at stake for them, what's driving it all.

The original folk version of *Snow White* came into the hands of the Grimm brothers in the early 1800s and, through them, was passed around on a wider scale than it had yet known. The Evil Queen served for a couple hundred years as a cautionary tale set against not the patriarchy but the absurd and selfish desires of older women. In the folk version, the Queen's bad behavior ends when her feet are plunged into red hot shoes and she dances herself to death; in Disney's version she's chased off a cliff by the seven dwarfs. Misogyny stays behind the curtain and is never revealed as the real culprit in this story. Because vanity is one of the seven deadly sins against God, there's hell to pay for indulging in it. And that's supposed to be that.

Immersed in the status quo, my childhood self had witnessed a Disney queen engaged in a competition she couldn't win, but as a mature woman I saw her stuck in a struggle against values she didn't create. To conclude, as children do and as I once had, that the Queen was self-serving and wrongheaded was to assume all the values in her world were exactly as they should have been. Blaming vanity is a different kind of wrong turn.

Vanus, meaning void, is the Latin adjective that's the source of the words *vain*, *vanity*, and *vanish*, and these words ride on the wings of an older Norse word *vanta*: to be lacking, to want. According to a discussion on Twitter by the linguist Danny Bate (@DannyBate4), "All of these also share a common root with *wanian*, to diminish, which is the ancestor of the (now rare) verb *wane*." To be seen or to see yourself as empty, used up, waning and to experience the futility of wanting to reverse time can feel intensely hard and painful. This is an existential crisis caused by the culture we live in, not something to be viewed with scorn.

When I found myself identifying with the Queen instead of with Snow White, I felt free to take some time to recognize my own difficulties around what has happened to my appearance in old age, those wobbly days. I've been subject to the same messages about youth and beauty that started with fairy tales and continued on through my life. Plenty of women in my age range have taken those messages to heart—it's hard not to—and rushed to a secret room, usually to be found in a clinic, to take on the disguises available for aging faces.

I know women for whom freezing in time a version of themselves they like and don't want to see disappear is the answer. For many women, vanishing hurts, and they want to do all they can to postpone the pain of it. I can understand this, but I have less compassion for the cosmetic "anti-aging" industry that is happy to cash in on these vulnerable feelings to the tune of around twenty-five billion dollars a year, according to various sources. The industry stands ready to put all manner of bandages on our vulnerability (from *vulnus*, meaning wound), but of course this isn't out of good heartedness or even supply and demand. Its advertising is excellent at creating even more shame and fear around aging so that the money keeps flowing in. The shame and fear angle on aging has even created new markets. An article published in the *Washington Post* stated that Botulinum toxin, known as Botox, is now being used not only for wrinkles but as a *preventive* for wrinkling. The mandate against aging is so powerful that even women as young as twenty are trying to forestall the changes the passing years will bring to their faces. Women between twenty and thirty-five make up about 20 percent of all Botox recipients. The American Society of Plastic Surgeons reported that, in the United States, the use of Botox has risen 878 percent since the start of the twenty-first century. Men get these treatments too, but the majority of the people starting at a younger age are women.

You'd think there'd be a lot of scratching of heads, but in fact there's an opposite response: rounds of applause. One twenty-eight-year-old who used Botox to erase the faint lines on her forehead received over two million hits and scooped up peer converts to the procedure on her TikTok Botox journey.

Marie Southard Ospina, a body-positive writer on the younger end of the millennial generation, questioned the downside of vanity in an article for *Bustle* headlined, "If Vanity is Loving Yourself, I'm All For It." In equating the word with self-love, she points out the negatives that result from a lack of caring about yourself. Although she points to Christianity as the source of vanity's sinful reputation, she finds that non-Christians disdain it as well because of the excessive self-absorption that it implies. I appreciate the question she raises about who gets to draw the line with regard to excess. "How much pride or love for yourself are you allowed before it turns into the negative type of vanity? And how much is too little if you don't fancy being perceived as self-conscious or insecure?"

She's right. In what ancient volume on any cobwebbed shelf will we find a list of measurements for going too far? Although more and more young women may find themselves leaning toward Botox with no qualms, trying to turn back the clock can be especially tricky for older women. Hair dye seems to have moved from the vanity column to the wise-career-move column, but what about a facelift? Eyebrow lift? Fillers? Or more invasive body procedures that address everything from spider veins to the puffy belly that often comes with menopause? Lots of people speak out negatively about doing anything at all. Given all the scrutiny, it can be hard to find our own boundaries around changes that can be had for a pile of money, if you happen to have some extra thousands lying around.

Going to the gym or running or strength training are considered fine. These things fall under the healthy and fit banner. Trying to look young when you're not, though, is another matter. Although vanity is a tightrope walk for women of any age, it's common to witness the special disapproval reserved for the older woman who stretches one Botox treatment too far, one neckline too low, or one facelift too high. On the Internet, people express genuine glee about facelifts and Botox gone wrong for women beyond fifty.

Disparagement is loudest when older women who were once considered real beauties have the nerve to show up as older, or as wanting to maintain at least a portion of their status. In her mid-fifties, model Linda Evangelista was criticized in the press and ridiculed on social media because she sued a clinic over a botched procedure called *cold sculpting* that left lumps on her body. People derided her for being unable to "accept aging" and suggested she get counseling. Her friends in the modeling profession, however, rushed to her defense and tried to comfort her. They understood more clearly than anyone the beauty industry she worked for and what aging means within it. Similarly, the women who made updates of popular TV shows such as *Sex and the City* and *Friends* got criticized for showing aging faces and bodies.

It's not only from men and the media that older women can experience dismissal and judgment. In *Look Me in the Eye: Old Women, Aging and Ageism*, published in 1983, Barbara Macdonald was the first feminist writer, at least that I know of, to describe the emotional upset and the anger that can come with old age even within one's community of women.

On a women's march in Boston for Take Back the Night, Barbara, then sixty-five, was singled out by an activist monitor who thought she might be unable to keep up with other marchers because of her age. A seasoned activist herself, she felt strong and positive about her purpose there with the others that night, and yet because of her gray hair and wrinkles she was perceived as frail, judged as not knowing what she was getting into, and advised to reconsider her place in a crowd of women who were much younger.

Macdonald describes this incident and how it felt. She asserts that youth culture and the patriarchy work together to keep old women in what is perceived to be their place, indistinguishable one from the other, servile at best. She reminds us of how the entire system works: "There can be no leisure elite consuming class unless it is off the back of someone." Then she points to what the partnership between patriarchy and youth culture actually means. She correlates the insistence on this one-up and one-down way of seeing things to what she learned from her experience as an old woman both observing and participating in feminism's second wave, primarily in white culture: "The older woman is who the younger women are better than—who they are more powerful than." Maybe because the young don't have much political power, they find at least some comfort in feeling better than someone, but she advises younger women to be aware that, if this continues, assumptions about them will also one day be made and those assumptions will be wrong, but it will be hard for an invisible person to step forward and make the truth known about herself.

Barbara Macdonald wrote her warning about what was going to happen if we didn't heed her message *forty years* ago. Most of the women who were young feminists, including me, continued on as if she hadn't sounded any warning at all. Many continued to use jokes, ridicule (even self-ridicule as aging progressed), and ageist remarks to try to shake off their own fears around getting old. *Anti-aging* became a common term in our language. What better term could there be for turning a body that's growing old into an enemy? Is this so different from the Queen who can't stop for a second to see where her feelings were coming from? She, poor thing, is stuck in a fairy tale, but the rest of us aren't.

Several years ago, when I first tried to share my thoughts about ageism on social media, the response, even among women over sixty, was either lukewarm or dismissive, often from the very feminists who caught on to their own oppression due to sexism when they were young. In my youth, I wanted freedom from expectations; as an older woman, I wanted freedom from the ideas around what a person my age should be, and I wanted to still count, and said so. I may have welcomed stepping out of the line of the male gaze, but that didn't mean I wanted to step out of the community of life altogether. I wondered why so many others didn't feel the same way, or at least why they weren't expressing it. I had a couple thousand friends on Facebook, quite a lot of them women of my own generation and slightly younger. Didn't it make them angry that we should be expected to accept a new list of expectations, this time around our own aging, all of which were held and perpetuated by people who'd simply inherited them, as we had? Didn't they want to read a new book I'd come across on women and aging that was bursting with facts and insights? Or a thoughtfully written essay about caregiving an elderly parent? Or a news report on the costs of ageism in medical care or anything else about aging and ageism that I posted now and then? Not really, at least not at first. This is changing. "But I don't *feel* old" is still often held up as a shield against the vulnerability being old can bring.

That expression always reminds me of how, in those early days of the second wave of feminism, many women denied oppression: "But I don't *feel* oppressed." In my community at that time, most feminists were enrolled in college and identified as straight whether we were or not. We heard about boyfriends and husbands who were "exceptional" and didn't oppress any women, let alone the ones they were with. This just happened to apply to almost every boyfriend or husband any woman in any consciousness-raising group had at the time. Thousands upon thousands of extraordinary young men who'd somehow escaped the culture's baked-in sexism must have populated all the campuses in the United States in the 1960s and 1970s. Still, whether acknowledged in boyfriends or anywhere else, sexism, which was unrelated to privilege, including the privilege of college, had by then long been a detrimental presence in all of our lives.

It angered me then when someone suggested we ignore sexism, and it upsets me now when an older woman, often a proud feminist, tells me, as some have done, to forget about all this ageism stuff and I'll be happier, as if ageism, unlike sexism, is a personal thing you can choose to shrug off. But when I ask if the same sorts of things are happening in their lives as are happening in mine, they often respond with detailed examples. Clearly, they are noticing it. Closer examination would seem to show that ageism is part of the culture, not personal, but this can be a hard conversation.

All those years ago as a student and beyond, I'd explored how sexist attitudes function in society, and I had watched the evolution of consciousness in myself and many around me. Thankfully, as the years have passed and I've stayed with social media, right or wrong, awareness has begun to shift around ageism, too, but it often feels slow going. "Get a sense of humor," was the essence of one remark from a woman in her sixties who had solicited my social network friendship but didn't like the fact that I posted articles about ageism, and it irked her that I'd complained about ageism in the greeting cards for older people, which turned out to be the very cards she liked to purchase. Hideous looking caricatures of old bodies meant to be laughed at didn't bother her a bit (*she* doesn't look like *them*), but sexist jokes and cartoons meant to show the silliness or stupidity of women set her on fire.

It often takes me a long time to accept things, too. I certainly didn't accept what Barbara Macdonald had to say in *Look Me in the Eye* when I first came across it many years ago. Now, though, when I watch myself and other women buy in to myths about aging faces and bodies, I realize what it has cost the majority of us to ignore her and then forget her. Striving to gain approval for physical selves that have been more or less written off by the larger culture is uncomfortable both to experience and to witness. There may be many reasons for us to post glamorous photos of ourselves when we turn fifty, sixty, or seventy, but I think some of us, consciously or not, may be using these images as a way to stand before a community mirror and invite reassurance. Dozens, if not hundreds, of followers and friends often whisper back some combination of the correct magic words in the comments: *You look great! Not a day over thirty! How beautiful you are! You don't look your age! No one would ever know you're seventy!*

Thank you, thank you, thank you, comes the relieved response.

Wanting to maintain an attractive self, fit and healthy and interesting to look at or even beautiful is no crime. The part I don't like in myself and bristle at when I see it in others is the belief that our age is an enemy. Reassurance from others may make us believe that whatever we're doing to fight this supposed enemy is paying off, for the moment anyway, but it's also—whether intended or not—reassurance that we still hold worth in the kingdom. It *is* still a kingdom, one that places youth and beauty for women among its highest values, and therefore one that owns us for as long as we subscribe to those values. When we make an appeal to be told that we are still *young* looking and get what we're asking for, we're cooperating in shutting out those who are not only old but *look* old and *feel* old. They, not we, remain *other*. In the kingdom, that rule will persist, and the drive a woman feels to stay young looking for as long as she can—if she's doing it for the sake of applause and approval and to be worthy of esteem—will remain strong. The *other* will remain other, too.

Old age is not another country we need to be well-armed to enter but an expansion of the borders of the homeland we've lived in all our lives, our bodies. Aging is personal. Each of us can make her own specific list of what we're losing, what we've lost—subtract something here, add something there. All the vanity on earth, even with its industrial partners, cannot keep pace with this, any more than the physical changes that faced us as children or adolescents or young adults or middle-aged people could have been stopped.

We know our bodies. They're not hostile environments. We've cared for them; dressed, fed, and groomed them; exercised them; given them pleasures great and small; taken them out for many spins in a multitude of uncharted territories. Should we reject them now because they're following, as they have been following all along, their own natural paths? The other day as I thought about this, I remembered my years as a preschool teacher and the way Mister Rogers talked to children about how to live a successful life: "The first way is to be kind. The second way is to be kind. The third way is to be kind." This is good advice at any time in our lives.

My mother paid careful attention to her clothes, her hair, her make-up, even into late old age. Alice was still using "anti-aging" cream during the hundredth year of her life, her last year. All along the way she exercised, ate very carefully, tried to take care of the things she could still control. To be seen as beautiful was important to her, and she did not enjoy her face and body changing with old age. With me, she felt free to complain, and I listened. To live to one hundred years is a long road and she'd learned a lot, but in her case, the pedestal of beauty she'd stood on for most of her life was a tall one. To look, for many decades, the way male preferences applaud you for looking made her old age a hard time. Yet, just as she'd found ways through pain and disabilities that came with advanced years, she found a way to work with it.

Alice lived at an assisted living facility for her last seven years. During that time I watched her, along with several other women, speak to their peers over and over again in positive ways, kind ways, about many things—the attractive lines of a new pair of glasses, a consistent flair for choosing anything from an interesting accessory to an interesting topic of conversation, the gift of always bringing levity to group gatherings, a talent for singing or piano, a strong handshake, a welcoming tone of voice, a sense of rhythm, a commitment to including others, a distinctive walk. These remarks were never flattery doled out to feed vanity. Despite any vanity any of them may still have been stuck with thanks to the times they'd grown up in, what my mother and these other women provided for one another was a real mirror, one in which they could reflect back real reasons they appreciated each other. They kept to the truth and used only a few words, a nod, a touch. They underscored strengths and drew attention to what all the years could not stop from shining through. They did it in order to bring each other into view and to articulate what they saw: Something interesting or lovely or graceful about you has caught my attention. In doing this, they acknowledged both the need for approval, a feature of the system they'd all grown up in, right or wrong, along with the simple need of all humans to feel validated.

All residents of these facilities, most of them female, once stood before mirrors and were affirmed as singular and present. Vanity may sometimes rise when visibility falls, but a very good thing I noticed about this form of community living is that sometimes it takes a village to raise up an old woman and give her back to herself. Sometimes social media can do this, too, even though it tends to favor an emphasis on appearances and big accomplishments.

Death, leaving this place we know so well, may be on the horizon, but that doesn't mean other things can't be in view while we're still here. I felt sad at how deeply my mother grieved what she saw as the loss of her beauty, but I learned from her practice of acknowledging others and have used it both with peers and people senior to me since she died, including strangers I see in the grocery store, at the post office, in line at the bank, anywhere, and I've noticed other older people use it with me, too. You don't need to seek out the mirror's approval when this validation is offered.

Sharing what we see about one another means we haven't vanished, we're perfectly visible, and, more importantly, it means that we *want* each other to be visible. Practicing this myself is one of the ways—and an unexpected one—that I keep my mother alive and with me. It's also the perfect antidote to my own fears of vanishing. For the time that I'm here I can bring something of value to interactions even with strangers, and as I get older I seem to be willing to talk to strangers more and more.

Is it foolish to hope that small but bright moments like these will increase among the general population, too? I want to believe that those among the young who now try so hard to exclude and put down the old in order to feel one-up on someone will stop doing that, and that the old will no longer try to one-up each other based on how good they look. It could happen if the demand for inclusiveness continues. I want to believe that each succeeding generation will perceive even more about what it means to be human, more to draw into the light and celebrate.

The Queen was pitted against one particular young person. I think if we could calm her down long enough to have a cup of tea and a chat, she might admit that the problem wasn't Snow White at all but something much larger, and it can change. An expansion of our ideas about the stuff beauty and grace are made of would be revolutionary.

Look at Me

News arrived that a short story of mine, in which the main character is a woman in her seventies, had been accepted by a literary magazine. I'd loved many of the pieces in this magazine's pages and respected the consistent beauty of its layout. I couldn't wait to see what sort of art would accompany my story, but when I clicked open the file for the review proof, I felt a little jolt in my stomach.

In the story, I'd described the woman, a retired attorney, as dressing with the flair she'd longed for after years of wearing dull suits in law offices and courtrooms. She wasn't after the extreme "advanced style" of a handful of East Coast older women but instead a muted though still colorful version. I'd written her clothing with care because it speaks to the woman she is now in her life and she knows and cares about the difference. A button from her jacket even plays a key part in the story.

Although I couldn't ask for any sort of specific rendition of my central character from a magazine that uses artists and not story illustrators to enhance the text, I hadn't expected to open the pages and find a painting of a dowdy woman with her arms and legs crossed and her whole body pulled inward. Her dreary clothes said not much other than Generic Old Woman.

I asked the editor to reconsider this choice and gave her my reasons. Thankfully, she changed it to something else. I wouldn't have thought any more about it, but not long after that I opened a fresh copy of the *New Yorker* and found a Lore Segal story with a similar issue. "Ladies' Lunch" relates a painful time in the life of a woman in her early eighties. Due to changes in her health and behavior, Lotte's sons want to move her out of her comfortable apartment, with its view of the Empire State Building, and even out of the city, far away from her close group of friends, also in their eighties. These women lunch together once a week. They know one another's lives inside out and rely on their connection. Her friends want to help Lotte but can't.

The story captured an issue for so many people no longer able to care for themselves, leaving home and friends behind. But this has become a common topic for stories about older people. What I appreciated about Segal's story was her realistic portrayal of the inability of the friends to help. Showing the power of family rising over the power of friends in late life is honest. In old age, it doesn't matter if you're closer to your friends than to family members because, in so many cases, family members determine what's "best" for you.

In the *New Yorker's* illustration, a woman with gray, permed hair sits in a taxi wearing a heavy brown sweater that looks like the one my grandmother wore back in the 1950s on the coldest days of North Dakota winters. Her face turns away as she looks out the cab window at a New York neighborhood. She reminded me of the oldest member of television's *The Golden Girls*. Based on this artwork, I'd originally thought the story would take place several decades in the past, but "Ladies' Lunch" is about a woman of these times, our times, in her early eighties.

I tried to imagine a short story in the *New Yorker* about a forty-something woman of today dealing, for example, with issues around getting funding for a marijuana dispensary. How would forty-something readers feel if the illustration showed a woman with a mullet haircut wearing clothes from the 1980s: a blazer with big shoulder pads and stirrup pants, glitter jellies on her feet? Wouldn't they be a little puzzled? Although nobody could open a marijuana dispensary in that decade, would the readers shrug off the art? *Oh, that's how we forty-year-old women look, I guess.*

Why do we accept an out-of-date representation of ourselves passively even though we know the appearance of a woman in old age changes from generation to generation, and old age itself ranges from sixty, which some who study aging call "young old age," to a very old one hundred plus, or "old old age?" Each stage of aging through these years brings alterations that differ person to person. We know these things because we are these people.

With a little digging, I discovered that the artists for my story and Segal's were both middle-aged men. I found a photograph in the online issue of the *New Yorker* showing Lore Segal herself at eighty-nine, her age when the story was published. She looked at least ten years younger than the woman in the illustration. Lotte, the character, was meant to be eighty-two. In her photograph, Segal appeared to be a woman approaching her nineties, that is, a woman born in the late 1920s, not the early 1880s, which is what the illustration offered.

No fictional story about an older person should call for an illustration resembling the author, of course, but it would have been simple enough for the artist to have taken a look at some contemporary women in their eighties. Given increased longevity, these women are all around us, easy to spot.

As a younger person, with the exception of knowing my own grandmother and the grandmothers of a few friends, I didn't think very deeply about the old as a generation that carried a generation's style. I'd certainly never thought about how the old were represented in art. These young male artists weren't much different in their understanding than I'd been at their age. I mentioned the Segal story art and the art for my story to a few friends and then put my thoughts about them aside. Things would change. They had to.

Denial worked until one day a lecture titled "Women in Power" on YouTube smashed it to bits. I watched as the lecturer, Professor Mary Beard, demonstrated a way to look at representation more closely. Her talk spurred me on to revisit how the old woman is currently represented and why.

At the start of her lecture, in her jovial, relaxed, and friendly way, and probably wearing the sparkly sneakers I'm told she's famous for, Professor Beard points out that if we close our eyes and try to conjure the image of a president or political leader, a mental picture of a male is most likely to pop to mind. She goes on to discuss her own environment, the academy (Newnham College, Cambridge), and says that even she would, at first, be likely to imagine someone male in the role of professor because that's the template she received, along with the rest of us.

To see if she was right about this being more or less typical of the imagination's response to the word "professor," she decided to google "cartoon professors." She chose cartoon images because she wanted to make sure she was looking at pictures quickly conjured up, not the ones we might actually see in real life or photographs. In other words, what picture does the mind immediately grasp as *professor* the moment we see it?

Out of the first one-hundred images for professors the search revealed, only one was a woman, and she was wearing slacks. Dr.

Beard then mentioned the pantsuits female politicians have been known to wear and described that women seeking office tend to lower the timbre of their voices in a conscious or unconscious echo of the predominance of males in leadership roles. She was off and running: women in power.

I paused the video and thought about Professor Beard's use of the word "template," *the templates we receive.* Her search for "cartoon professor" gave me an idea. I typed "cartoon old woman" into the search box on Google.

Nothing could have prepared me for the excess of images showing an old person with her hair in a bun. A few pictures showed old women exercising, which I thought was a good thing, but don't think you'll escape a bun with body movement: buns in the yoga studio, buns on the run, buns here, there, and everywhere. I did a quick scan down the page. Bun after bun after bun flew by. Out of the first one-hundred images, forty-nine of these cartoon old women wore their hair in a bun. In real life, it's plain to see that one out of every two women over the age of sixty doesn't wear her hair in a bun. The bun can be a handy way to tuck long hair away. I do this sometimes myself, though it's more likely to be half bun, half ponytail in my rush to get it out of my face. But the style of bun shown in most of the images is a remnant of times gone by when women could not cut their hair even if they wanted to, even if they were very old and tired of washing that "virginal" mane year in and year out. In Google image land, the Victorian era rules, and this style is a template drawn upon for "old woman" more than a hundred and fifty years later.

Thirty-three of the cartoon women in those first one-hundred images used canes. I once had to use a cane after taking a serious fall a few weeks before my sixty-fifth birthday. For the months I used it, I felt grateful to have it, but I rarely saw anyone else with a cane. Nobody in my aging neighborhood or in my aging workplace, except for me, used one. When I went into the city for various appointments or to shop, I hardly ever saw anyone close to my age with a cane. (When you're dependent on one yourself, you notice.) Yet, at the time I checked Google, cartoon images showed three out of every ten older people reliant on a cane.

Many of the cartoon old women were white, and sedentary. Lots of them were obese, bent, misshapen, or all three. If a bun was not pictured, then an old-fashioned curly perm replaced it. The close, tight perm hasn't been popular for anyone over fifty since at least my mother's generation, and she was born in 1915. Often, the woman in the images wore an article of clothing from a previous century, the twentieth if she was lucky. Only four out of the one hundred images struck me as looking remotely contemporary.

"We have no template for what a powerful woman might look like except that she probably looks rather like a man," Mary Beard had said in her lecture. It was bad enough to think of male artists filling the pages of magazines with illustrations of older women from previous eras, but I couldn't deny an almost physical ache of frustration when I thought of people conjuring one of the cartoon images that filled my laptop screen when they closed their eyes and thought "old woman." It wasn't that canes, walkers, and bent bodies should be excluded. They should be there, as should hair in a bun and maybe even the occasional throwback perm. But defaulting to these stereotypes for "old woman" is as dishonest as assuming all professors are male.

What *does* an old woman look like? When I look in the mirror, I see myself first, of course, but if I muster some objectivity I see a woman well advanced in years, someone who came of age in the 1960s, not the 1880s, which is when my great-grandmother was a young woman, the same decade the cartoon women would have been young. These two very different eras account for differences in hairstyle and wardrobe, including shoes and eyeglasses, to name the most obvious changes. They account for skin that looks less wrinkled, too, thanks mostly to widespread use of sunscreen.

When I look at my close friends who were born within about ten years of me, of course I see beloved faces, but I also see the faces of older people. When I scan through my Facebook friends list, multitudes of aging faces pass by, each unique and each uniquely contemporary. In my neighborhood, older faces and bodies are visible up and down the moorage. What I'm least likely to see anywhere is the woman of the template: the bun, the cane, the frizzy perm, the clothing from another century—all the go-to images that illustrators grab onto for a quick message.

The caricatures showing people in a certain age demographic as out of touch, out of style, and odd are damaging to a giant slice of the population in the same way that stereotypical and denigrating images are to any group of people. Instead of what we can see with our own eyes if we care to look, we're constantly being trained to fall back on mental pictures, cartoon and otherwise, that steer us away from reality. As long as our minds present us with laughable, unreal, or skewed visual pictures, we don't have to feel anything when tapping out condemnations of all "boomers" on Twitter feeds or blaming the old for a lockdown while a pandemic rages. When COVID swept through nursing homes, how many images like these came to people's minds and made those losses easier to dismiss? Good-bye to all those weird-looking, frizzy-haired people. Unless you know one personally and happen to love her, who cares?

※ ※ ※

For almost a dozen years after college graduation, I taught pre-school. The experience reinforced a passion for picture books that began with my Aunt Mattie, a children's librarian, reading to me early on. My book collection thinned out as friends and neighbors with children and grandchildren started to look for books. I gave many away. Sometimes I'd donate a stack to a thrift store in an effort to downsize. But after the Mary Beard lecture and the Google image search, I pulled out what was left and, off and on for several days, looked at illustrations.

I still had a few nursery rhyme books and some folk and fairy tales in which old women appear, many of them poor. This made me think of the way, early in our lives, we're taught to link old age with poverty, and of the fact that being poor is still very much a reality for many who are old, especially women. I'd recently looked at a report from Justice in Aging, an organization dedicated to fighting senior poverty by means of the legal system. In 2020, 45 percent of Americans over sixty-five were having trouble meeting their basic needs.

I put the folk and fairy tales aside to focus on more modern-day children's stories, supplementing my own collection with online searches for stories with older women, some of which allowed me to page through the story online and see how the old woman is presented. The first thing I noticed was wardrobe. As in the cartoons, an awful lot of these characters are either wearing clothes long out of style or completely wacky. Some of them bear outsized heads and small bodies, while others have large bodies and small heads. So many illustrations seemed to be encouraging small children to find the old humorous and unreal.

In one book, a child close to his grandmother becomes fearful of losing her when she starts dating a man he doesn't know, a reasonable premise for a young child's story. What seems odd to me is that the grandmother's clothing changes from comfortable to bright and tight, and yes, up goes her hair into a sort of bun.

Nana isn't attending a costume party. She's going out on a date. Why should she be made to look comical and to suffer from bad taste? Meanwhile, the boy looks and dresses like a normal kid throughout the story. The theme is poignant but the message coded into the images is clear: Poor silly Nana.

I Know an Old Lady Who Swallowed a Fly is another book in which the old woman in the story becomes an almost curious object. My preschool kids had laughed at this ridiculous rhyme where the fly that's swallowed is followed by a spider, a bird, a cat, a goat, and more and more odd things no one could possibly swallow. It's this absurdity that makes the children laugh, plus the refrain "I guess she'll die," because the very idea of death is hilarious to small children. Most of them don't know what it means, and anyway it has nothing to do with them.

The old lady in my copy was flat faced and wretched looking but not as hideous as she is in some of the later versions. I began to think the illustrators had entered some sort of contest to make the character as revolting as possible—as if the funny part is her, not what she's doing. Can't a person swallow a hideous and hairy fly without being hideous and hairy herself?

I was surprised to see that the popularity of the rhyme has brought forth new books about unsightly old ladies swallowing everything under the sun: leaves, bats, roses, the moon. Illustrators not only dress these women in peculiar ways but make them look fundamentally unsound, and I know at least one of them is not unsound because many times I have looked up at the night sky and wanted to swallow the moon, especially the harvest moon. *If only.*

In one of the most well-known and well-loved children's books of the last thirty years, every single aged person residing in the care home next door to a little boy's house looks like an alien life form. Once again, throughout the story, the little boy looks like a little boy.

Each image in this book may be interesting for a child to pore over, but all of the older people in the story come across as peculiar, though all peculiar in the same way; they are *other*, definitely not in the same human category as the boy. As the stand-in for the child reader, he wanders among strange beings with bodily distortions and weird faces, all of whom wear strange, sloppy clothing.

The little boy is kind. He helps one of the residents regain memories dear to her. The story has more heart than the illustrations. Are we supposed to think this is how children truly see or want to see old people? It doesn't matter. This is how we are telling children who read this book to see old people. The woman with memory loss, gets sympathy. The others seem to belong on a different planet.

Though its message of compassion about memory loss is valuable, I wonder whether young parents who buy this book think about the way it depicts older people. Perhaps they were raised on similar images. Goodreads shows the faces of the people writing their reviews. In the case of this particular book, a lot of people who seem to be somewhere between twenty and forty are reviewing it. Some of them discuss the book as parents, some as teachers, some as both, and others don't mention why they read it.

There are reviews that don't discuss the art, but often it is praised. The word "beautiful" comes up a lot. One woman appreciates the fact that they show "elastically challenged socks, multicolored dresses, and baggy pants." To her, I guess, these things equal *old*. Another describes the images as "cartoonlike and accurate in an interesting way." Is that possible? She then goes on to support this by telling us that older people in the story are "overweight, have wrinkles, wear glasses, and wear commonly worn clothes for people at an old age home." Only one review that I found on Goodreads—I didn't look at them all but read several random pages—describes the images as "garish and kind of creepy." Otherwise, it's all "wonderful, joyous illustrations," "kid friendly and adorable," and so on.

Yes, the story's message is worthwhile, but I wonder how many grandparents who buy this book stop to ask themselves how they want to be perceived by their grandchildren, how they want their peers to be perceived, and, as importantly, how they want their grandchildren to see themselves as they grow older. I hope at least some of them consider asking their grandchildren why they think the old people in the story don't look as human as the little boy does. There's a worthwhile conversation that could come from that question.

I felt lucky when I found books that didn't put older women in baggy or clownish clothes. *Grandma's Purse* by Vanessa Brantley-Newton is an intergenerational story in which both of the main characters dress normally. Grandmother and granddaughter go through the grandmother's purse together. The way they bond over the purse's contents feels more real because of this. In *Aunt Flossie's Hats (and Crab Cakes Later)* by Elizabeth Fitzgerald Howard and illustrated by James Ransome, an older woman's collection of hats brings back memories that she shares with her visiting nieces. *North Woods Girl*, by Aimee Bissonette, illustrated by Claudia McGehee, is the story of a girl who visits her grandmother and joins her for seasonal walks through the forest the grandmother knows well because she lives there.

Sometimes historic clothing is appropriate to the story, and when it is, it's accurate and interesting. *Miss Moore Thought Otherwise* tells the story of Anne Moore, who started a children's library in New York and then, in her seventies, traveled across the country to make other children's libraries possible. This picture book gives children not only beautiful illustrations but a glimpse at a full life well lived, an old woman they can look up to and be grateful for. *Miss Rumphius* by Barbara Cooney is another picture book showing an old woman first as a child and then through her life and into old age. What comes across clearly in these two books is that we are the same people when old as we were when young. Some things change, but the important and essential parts of us do not. It's a pleasure to see that the clothing on the old women in each of these books is appropriate to their time.

Because of those preschool teaching years and because I've had the opportunity to know many children, I'm aware that whimsy in the wardrobe department can be purposeful in a picture book. Some children can identify with a character who has a strong desire to wear whatever she wants to wear, and maybe unlike the child who is holding the book, the character gets away with it. There's a vicarious thrill children can take in that freedom. I can't think of a good reason ridiculous clothing should become the default style for the old woman, though. There's no default style for other generations in picture books, and with the examples above, it's clear that it's easy to create wardrobes both true to the spirit of the character and her times.

I found one book in which an older woman's clothes communicated something interesting, not foolish, about her. In *The Old Woman Who Named Things* by Cynthia Rylant, illustrated by Kathryn Brown, the main character wears rolled-up pants, cowboy boots, and vests. At first this clothing seems a little eccentric, but then along comes a page that shows her in an old photograph, a child with a horse, and she's dressed the same way. It's satisfying to see that she remains true to the spirit of the child she once was. Yes, her clothes might look strange to someone out of context. Most children, though, look closely at the illustrations in a book.

And that, I thought, as I put my books and laptop away after examining many old woman illustrations, is the point. Children look closely.

My research was not sweeping, and I realize I made only an informal dive into what is out there. I found enough evidence, though, to feel sad about the state of things and to regret any stories I'd read to young kids that showed old women and old men, too, as odd. Back in the 1970s and 1980s when I taught, we teachers were becoming more aware of racism and sexism in books, but not ageism.

The oldest students of my former preschool classes are in their fifties now. What negative images might they be carrying around as they approach their own old age, planted in those early days when they were forming their first ideas about people? I wondered if they were dyeing their hair and cursing their wrinkles and their changing bodies. Luckily, I'd been trained at one of the best preschools in the country, at the University of Iowa, and it contained a large picture book library chosen by a group of educators who'd spent a lot of time thinking about the minds and needs of preschool-age children, so I hoped we'd done well by them for the most part. But then again, picture books were only the beginning of the messages they were bound to hear about the unworthiness of being old.

Curious to learn more, I came across quite a few online scholarly papers written by researchers interested in how the old in stories are made to show up for children. As far back as 1981, reading specialists were encouraging teachers to look at old age and its representation in books. "Ageism in Literature: An Analysis Kit for Teachers and Librarians," sponsored by the Department of Education, gives a basic understanding of what's at stake. Reba Ouimet wrote an English honors essay titled "A Grimm Reminder: Representations of Female Evil in the Fairy Tales of the Brothers Grimm." An article published in *Journal of Children and Media* reports on an improvement in images, even though it also includes the fact that there isn't much improvement in how often older characters of substance are part of a story.

Best of all, I found an active website, A is for Aging, that reviews books for young children with ageism specifically in mind, along with multiculturalism and intergenerational exchange. This site was created by Lindsey McDivitt, a health educator and children's book author (*Nature's Friend: The Gwen Frostic Story*). When I contacted her to tell her how much I appreciated the site, she told me about her impressions of picture books when she started out several years ago after deciding to write books for children herself. "I read so many and I was quite horrified by the images of aging I stumbled upon," she said. "It was obvious that authors, editors, and publishers were buying into aging myths and aiming to pluck on heartstrings, not show aging accurately."

Now, years into the project, she has noticed a change in publishing, but it doesn't go far enough. "There has been a huge push to address diversity of all kinds in books for kids—such as race, ethnicity, religion, and gender. But the children's literature community has still not fully recognized the fact that aging is also diverse."

On her website, educators, librarians, parents, and grandparents can find books that contain positive and widely varied images of aging. Many of the books specifically feature grandmothers and grandchildren. I regularly order books she recommends as gifts for friends with children or grandchildren. New templates are being offered to young children. We only have to look for them. What children take away from these books will help shape their lives. There's a chance that they can not only become adults with compassion and understanding, but eventually become older people who will take the humanity of the old for granted.

My story that was almost published with an inappropriate illustration, "The Old Woman and the Boy," is about a meeting in a train station between two people who sense a great distance between themselves based on their ages but who ultimately choose to connect anyway. I like to think that other people out there are blowing on this little spark of hope that we can engage so much more meaningfully when we allow one another full status.

Winter's Tales

When I was a child and could finally read on my own, I found myself immersed in books filled with characters who seemed more or less like me in that they encountered strangeness, dangers, wonder, the fantastic, and the ordinary on a more or less daily basis. Children in these books employed pluck, wit, and their wits to gain hard-won triumphs. Every word flowed easily from these pages to my brain. I found comfort, affirmation, and sometimes the uncomfortable but honest validation that life is painful. Old Yeller does die, after all, as does Charlotte, even after saving Wilbur's life with her web craft.

Around age nine or ten, I discovered Tom Sawyer and Huck Finn, Pip of *Great Expectations*, and Jim Hawkins of *Treasure Island*— all boys, but at least the stories addressed my own hunger for adventure. Their longings matched mine, even overmatched them, giving me something to reach for. As girls and women have done over centuries of literature about male heroes, I mentally donned their clothes and merged my heart with theirs.

By twelve, I'd read every book of interest to me in the children's department of the small library in Pipestone, Minnesota, one of several small towns we lived in when I was growing up. My standards changed as I felt my internal compass take a big swing. A true North glimmered somewhere beyond my imagination. I needed stories about what and where and how, but at the time there was no category called young adult literature. I could feel a monumental experience headed my way, but I couldn't find any guideposts in the kinds of books I'd been reading.

Around that time, Bernice, the children's librarian, handed me a copy of *Little Women*. Jo March, a tomboy who liked writing skits and plays, the same as I did, walked into my imagination, showing me new possibilities. But after I'd read that book, Bernice had no more to offer. She shrugged and quickly scribbled a note. She pointed me upstairs to the adult library, instructing me to give her message to the librarian there.

I rushed up the wide wooden steps, leaving children's classics, magic spells, horse stories, dog stories, and girl detectives behind. Once in the adult library, my first pick was *Auntie Mame* by Patrick Dennis, and it had me in stitches. I felt excited about the madcap life awaiting me as a grown-up. More loans from the adult book department, along with shelves of best-selling novels left by the previous owners of a house my family moved into the following year, sobered me right up.

Many of the books I read over the next ten years, thanks to the guidance of high school English teachers and college literature professors, gave form to youthful experience and expanded my understanding of who I was and what I wanted: *To Kill a Mockingbird, The Haunting of Hill House, The Diary of a Young Girl, Emma, Giovanni's Room, The Heart Is a Lonely Hunter, Their Eyes Were Watching God, The Waves, The Bell Jar,* and many more plays, short stories, and novels that had been carefully selected with the intention of helping young people explore their own humanity and learn how to think.

Through the years following, thanks to reading book reviews

and making friends with people who read a lot, I also found someone I could identify with over and over again in novels about young or middle-aged protagonists experiencing love, betrayal, loss, missed connections, shattered marriages, frustrated careers, marches across Germany, imprisonments in Russia, wars everywhere, colonization, rebellions, camel rides across deserts, alcohol and drug addiction, persecution, prosecution, corruption, uprisings, towns without pity, and more. I donned imaginary clothes countless times and always learned something about myself when occupying these worlds because of course there was always something in the main character that I recognized, something that would carry me through the story.

I never dreamed this powerful stream of stories that spoke to my experience would become a mere trickle when I reached old age, but it did. Isaac Bashevis Singer wrote, "Literature has neglected the old and their emotions. The novelists never told us that in life, as in other matters, the young are just beginners and that the art of loving matures with age and experience."

Once upon a time the chime above the door of my favorite bookshop meant a carefree right turn and a quick walk toward the table featuring new fiction. Which one or two would I choose with my monthly budget for books? Although good reviews tended to make me more curious about some than others, I had an open mind. The unheralded called to me, too, with their evocative covers and impressive blurbs. All in all, a feast of books.

These days I visit the little bookshop less frequently. It's a long drive from my houseboat into the city, a drive that involves increasingly hectic Portland traffic. Then, too, a pandemic has swept over us and people in my age range are at higher risk. Should I really ratchet up my stress levels and risk my life for a new book? Sometimes I do, and when I get there I always turn to the right, look for a novel or story collection about older women and usually don't find any such thing, pick up the well-reviewed novels, read the blurbs, sometimes even a few pages of text. Then, after this ritual, I very often put these books down again, one by one, and leave the table to go poke around other sections of the bookstore, wandering the aisles slightly dejected. When I leave, the chime above the door sounds less cheery than it did when I entered.

I feel the same when I stand before the new fiction shelf at the library. All the books there would have us believe that human life is all spring, summer, and maybe a few brisk days of fall. Few winter's tales line these shelves, and by this I mean honest stories in which an older man or, my special interest, an older woman, is the protagonist and the story is about this character experiencing life not as a flashback to her youth but from right there where she is: old age.

Sometimes a younger neighbor or acquaintance, aware of my unfathomable interest in novels about aging, will recommend a title that features older characters. Many are in the cozy mysteries category. I do like some of these, as millions of people do. Witness the popularity of the TV series *Murder, She Wrote* or all the Miss Marple stories by Agatha Christie. An online search for "senior sleuths" leads to a Goodreads list and other sites that feature what are called "cozies," with results often showing more contemporary authors. A murder in the village with a woman past fifty on the case—more power to her if she's got a quirk or two but can still outsmart the best detective the force has to offer—is still a surefire formula for a relaxing read. But these books don't give me the desired reflections on the later years of life itself I'm longing for.

My eyes tire easily these days, and for the remainder of my time I want to use them for books that matter to me. It's not that I want a steady diet of novels about women over sixty, but if I can find a good one, I'm going to choose to spend my book money and visual energy there rather than a cozy mystery or even on a novel about, say, a young woman heading from the Midwest to Paris, for example, or even a lighthearted story about a gang of postmenopausal women deciding to commit a few crimes together. I don't want the grandmother who dies early in the story either, leaving her young granddaughter to wrap up her life for her. If someone's going to hand me a book about a grandmother and small granddaughter, let it be as beautiful and true as Tove Jansson's *The Summer Book*.

This fact that older people as central figures are largely missing in literature adds to the sense of invisibility we often feel already, but it's not exactly something we can complain to the librarian about, or the bookstore manager either. What can they do but order the best books they can find in the publishers' catalogs, the ones they think will sell? So I go on thinking about it on my own and try to understand what this absence means and why it matters. In Isaac Singer's time, when he noticed the absence, maybe there wasn't a large audience for such stories, but these days I can't understand why publishers' catalogs aren't full of books that will appeal to older readers, given that this is a reading population and more than ten thousand people turn sixty-five every day, a fact that will continue for years to come. What are the acquisition editors thinking, the marketing staff, the editors themselves? A market exists.

Of course I can identify with characters in each and every good novel because literature mirrors the human condition and feeds our souls. It lets us know we're not alone, no matter how frightened we are that we might be. Sometimes I feel a keen pleasure when reading about young people and middle-aged people because I know what those ages felt like for me, and I'm moved by their innocence and wants and especially by their suffering, much of which I see is as avoidable for them as it was for me. I marvel at how hard we are on others and on ourselves, but also how necessary we are to each other, how sustaining. My heart can still lift when one more story reveals the depth of what it means to be human. Shouldn't I be satisfied with the reality of the literary world as it is? The soul is ageless, isn't it? And so why all this pining?

I can't help it. Even if I do find some recently published, highly touted, award-winning novel, take it home, and sit down to read it, and even if I've had an excellent reading experience and am enlightened a thousand fold when I'm done, I still hear a soft voice whisper, *Good enough, but where are our stories?*

If you're old and also a lesbian or person of color or someone with a disability or poor, or marginalized in other ways, your hope for a literary work that reflects you will sink on a regular basis. Even among the lion's share of the best recent novels, the answer to that question—where am I?—will too often be: *You? Oh, I didn't see you standing there, but now that you're pestering me let me ask, why would anybody want to read about you?*

Aging happens. It is so very real. Its stories are not the stories of youth, as many other cultures recognize. To suppose it isn't real enough to matter, or that it's real, all right, but too difficult and disturbing to take in, is to strike a line through a decade or two or three of our lives. In those years we do continue to exist, at the very least to ourselves and often to others. Shelves empty of literature about us and about the ways so many issues intersect with age do not reflect reality. Stories abound, just not in literature.

Ever since first hearing that voice in my head asking where our stories are, I've searched online now and then for good novels about this time of life. For a long time it was remarkable how quickly *The Old Man and the Sea* came bobbing up, as if the old fellow's marlin should be enough to feed us all for generations. Rarely was a novel with an old woman as the protagonist on any of these lists.

Years passed, and a few more stories started to show up on lists, notably books by established novelists of earlier generations. With the exception of Muriel Spark, who wrote the popular and well received *Memento Mori* when she was in her forties, most of the predominantly white authors included wrote about (white) women in old age when the novelists themselves were either in it or inching toward it: Margaret Drabble, Doris Lessing, May Sarton, Elizabeth Taylor, Barbara Pym, Leonora Carrington, Margaret Laurence, Angela Thirkell, and more. Even though I've read and liked most of the novels by the writers mentioned, I keep waiting for my own generation's voices, or those slightly younger, to be heard now, describing what it is to grow old in this era.

Perhaps an older writer who thinks about taking a chance on writing about her gray-haired sisters might consider it a little risky. She's already living on the edge. Fiction with male protagonists sells an average of ten million more copies than female protagonists (according to a recent report in BookRiot). Not only that, her work may often be overlooked in order to make room for the young woman writer. If you're a woman in the older novelist category, you might be aware of all those young female faces looking out at you from the pages of reviews and literary websites—even *People* magazine—each holding her first novel. Not all of these young women are geniuses; not even the majority are (and certainly not the majority of writers of any age are geniuses). It's their youth, not their genius, that calls for them to be featured. Still, no blame should fall on these younger writers just because the powers that be have deemed them and their first novels and their new faces worthy of attention. We want to hear new voices, too.

Besides, aging is not exactly considered a hot topic for novels. Headline writers for book reviews with older characters apparently recoil at the very thought of the subject matter. Even the most lauded writers can't dodge them: "Death and Disaster Stalk the Characters in Margaret Drabble's New Novel," shouted the headline in the *New York Times* review of *The Dark Flood Rises*. Cynthia Ozick wrote the review. Because she describes the book's themes and characters with intelligence and understanding, I suspect this headline was probably not her idea. Magda Szabó's novel, *The Door*, one of the most profound and enthralling novels about an old woman I've ever read (Szabó was approaching seventy when she wrote it), was heralded as a true bummer in the headline provided by the *New Yorker* in its review: "The Hungarian Despair of Magda Szabo's The Door." How many readers will look at these headlines and think, *I can't wait to read this book about an old woman and death and despair?*

Yet, some of us will read those headlines, as I did, and jump in anyway, figuring who better knows the score about older women than the older writer? Who else knows the range of stories there are about her to tell? And there's a lot of good news for the older novelist with an idea for an aging female protagonist in mind: old is new to us, the waiting readers. After a lifetime of drowning in male protagonists, how many more of them could we want? The older population has quadrupled since 1900 and is ever increasing; within that population people are living longer than ever before—more years available for reading. Furthermore, the newly old grew up reading the same way I did; those who read a lot and have money to buy books will buy them. They've been buying novels and borrowing them from libraries for decades now. Among this population, writers will likely find a hungry audience for stories describing what it is to come into this time of life. Everything comes down on the side of an older writer who wants to place an older person as a protagonist in her next novel.

Yet publishers seem to continue to think, mistakenly, there's no interest in a fictional compass for old age the same way they thought (and many still think) there's no interest in characters and stories about people who don't happen to be white. Maybe they believe that all we need to know about living past sixty can be found in nonfiction books by geriatricians and social scientists.

Or maybe publishers think the old writer is old first, with not much to say unless it's about her own past. We can find some memoirs that pull us into interesting pasts, like Diana Athill's *Stet*, for example. As a literary editor, she worked with many well-known writers and tells stories about Jean Rhys, V.S. Naipaul, Norman Mailer, and Philip Roth, among other famous names. Memoirs like hers satisfy the longing I feel, to some extent, and they can be beautifully written. Still others about lesser-known figures can be fascinating, too. Memoir writers now often use fictional techniques to infuse a story with a page-turning quality.

Still, fiction is a different kind of experience. Even if the writer of a memoir is not well known but has a good story to tell and even if that story resonates with our own experiences in life, it remains specifically the author's story. We may identify with this real person. We may cheer her on or feel the pain of her losses, as we do with fictional characters. But when we read fiction, I believe the story itself becomes even more our own. There's always been a contract between the storyteller and the listener, the author and the reader. The deal goes like this: the author disappears, not to be seen or heard from (except in rare cases and the asides to "Dear Reader" in some early fiction). The characters take over.

This illusion that there's no one pulling the strings, that a story stands on its own and belongs to no one else other than to the person reading it, frees the reader to become a character and to interpret things through that character's eyes, thereby transforming herself. Facts may exist in both fiction and a memoir, but the experience of reading them is different, at least it is for me. If I pick up the *New Yorker*, for example, and turn to any page, I almost always know immediately if I'm reading fiction or a nonfiction account of an experience. Nonfiction is an art, too, and I don't mean to take anything away from it. This book, after all, is nonfiction. But it's a different art. Similarly, a photograph may give us a view of a real place, whereas a painting, even if it's a painting of the same real place seen in the photograph, puts the viewer in that place imaginatively. Imagination isn't some random quality to be applied or not applied; it makes all the difference. It means the viewer experiences many different facets of that same place.

I wouldn't mind at all finding more well-written memoirs about women beyond a certain age, but my preference would be that such memoirs would not primarily be about the author's youth and would focus on what their life experience has been in the more recent past or her present, her mature life. Of course there are many, many stories of women's political and other history that should be preserved in memoirs, and I hope they will be.

When good literature—novels, stories, memoirs, plays, poems—about any group of people is missing, it leaves others not in that group to guess, to suppose, to rely on stereotypes, and to judge, often wrongly, as I talked about in the essay "Look at Me." Stereotypes will always make us dread any encounter with these suspicious folks, and we will try to push the people in that group off into the margins where we don't have to see them. As Zoe Brennan writes in her book, *The Older Woman in Recent Fiction* (McFarland & Company, 2005), "the category of woman remains incomplete" so long as older women are misrepresented or ignored in literature.

I didn't think much about how literary stereotypes of the old came into existence until reading *The Coming of Age* by Simone de Beauvoir. She wrote that the characteristics and attitudes of older people in literature for a long time have been taken from tropes about aging fed to the public by previous generations of writers. Early in the last century, for example, younger writers may not have known anyone over fifty or possibly sixty, not even their own grandparents, because lifespans were shorter. To construct an old character, writers dipped into the well of times gone by and pulled out qualities and even bodily conditions as if they still applied. This continues to this day, even when people who are seventy now may have nothing much more than wrinkles in common with someone who was seventy in 1920.

Despite the fact that our lifespans are longer and we've lived through extraordinary times of change, the assumption on the part of a reader may be that a novel about aging will be dreary. *Death. Disaster. Despair.* Who wants that? At the very least, some serious degree of bafflement about everything will show up. *Dementia.*

I think this particular expectation about dementia came about because a few good contemporary writers have taken an interest in it, and there are large numbers of readers who want novels on this subject, probably because it has cut close to home. It's as worthy a subject for fiction, after all, as a forty-something husband losing his marriage because of an affair, or a woman being held back time and again from a promotion. Being booted out of your own mind is just as hard a thing to reckon with than those life experiences, so why not write and read books about it? They can easily be found. Here are a few of many: *Still Alice; Elizabeth is Missing; Turn of Mind; Unbecoming; Goodbye, Vitamin; Three Things about Elsie; A Spool of Blue Thread; Stars Go Blue.*

But, as those of us who are older quickly discover, dementia isn't the only story about old age. Although the brain does change, dementia isn't a "normal" part of aging. Risk increases as we get older, but even among the oldest old (eight-five and older), not everyone suffers from dementia.

The only way we will become more visible to ourselves, to each other, and to younger readers is if we appear in works that show the full range of who we are, what we're like, what we do, and even what we can no longer do and fill our time with instead. "Growing, ripening, ageing, dying—the passing of time is predestined, inevitable," Simone de Beauvoir bluntly states in *The Coming of Age*, but this doesn't preclude, she goes on to say, "pursuing ends that give our existence meaning—devotion to individuals, to groups or to causes, social political, intellectual or creative work." More books about the reality of this time of life seem essential nurturing for both the old and the young. She writes: "If we do not know what we are going to be, we cannot know what we are: let us recognize ourselves in this old man or in that old woman. It must be done if we are to take upon ourselves the entirety of our human state."

No generation is ever going to be part of some generic "old woman" brand (and no old woman ever has been). The years that have formed us and the years we are experiencing now are distinct from the years that shaped all the women who preceded us. Many protagonists in our novels will see life through the perspective of feminism. They'll be based on the women who marched for LGBTQ rights—what would a character drawn from that population be doing now? Women who took on careers in every possible area of life, pushed hard at the boundaries of art, music, and literature, and gained access to both birth control and abortion are deserving subjects—what if we follow one or two or ten or a hundred or a thousand-plus characters like this through their days as lived now?

I wish I'd pick up a novel and find a woman who's decides to get a horse at the age of seventy or become an entrepreneur, or one who headed in her youth straight for suburbia and is still living that life in her sixties and wondering about her choices. I want to read the stories of the old woman who has been cleaning other peoples' houses, taking care of other women's elders, the one who joined a cult at forty and decides to leave it at sixty, the eighty year old knocking on doors to register voters, the sixty year old who fights the system on behalf of the immigrants who live next door, the abortion provider afraid to retire because there's nobody to replace her, the campaign adviser, the waitress, the street vendor, the gallery owner, the dog rescuer, the librarian without a library any more, the retired social worker who no longer has a way to help people, the woman who finds herself using a walker for the first time. Homeless old women who have to choose between pushing loaded carts up and down busy streets or being squirreled away in a daughter's spare bedroom—I want their stories. I want the stories of the artist who has never received much recognition in all her years of practicing her art and yet still practices it at sixty, seventy, eighty.

I don't think our stories need to be about the ninety-eight-year-old skydiver, the seventy-seven-year-old race car driver, the eighty-one-year-old long distance swimmer. Exceptionalism is fun to read about in a newspaper article or see on YouTube, but unless a character who does these things is fascinating in other ways, it's hard to imagine reading a whole novel about them. I'm happy for them, but these stories mislead us. Old age is interesting in the same ways other ages are interesting. Plenty of older people are busy with ordinary, revelatory, profoundly interesting, and challenging human matters: falling in love, caring for others, moving on, having sex, making music, building things, trying to get through a day with the minimum amount of pain or deal with the boredom that seeps in when everything and everyone is out of reach thanks to a pandemic. It's life, in other words, with this condition of old attached to it, as the ages of eighteen to twenty-four, for example, are life with the condition of young attached.

In my years of searching for narratives about aging, well over a decade now, I have found some interesting novels (see the appendix). They've given me the words to know and understand my own experience. Sometimes they've brought pleasure while also illuminating things I didn't want to see and yet knew were there and needed to be faced. I'm especially grateful for those writers who have done this in an artful and companionable way, inviting me to reflect truthfully on where I am now.

❋ ❋ ❋

One cold, gray October day, I was dreading the coming Portland winter: skies the color of steel wool and months of downpours. I'd spent a couple of hours at my computer writing and my body was hurting. I felt angry because I hadn't been sitting that long and the severe ache in my hips did not feel deserved for such a short time. Also, although they'd only been working for part of an afternoon, my eyes burned from the computer's light, even though it was in so-called "night mode." I stared out the window at the river feeling creaky and cranky and unprepared for either pouring rain or further bodily aging.

I decided to distract myself from the gloom with a happy project: I'd give the books in my living room a good dusting and place them back onto clean shelves. I'd no sooner started than my hand reached for a small volume, *Two Old Women*, a long-ago gift from a friend, a writer several years older than I who had died the previous January. Although she'd given it to me about a decade before, I'd never read it, had even forgotten I had it. Missing her and our many conversations about books, I sat down to read. By this short book's end, a couple of hours later, I felt deeply grateful for the gift.

Two Old Women is neither a novel nor a memoir but an imaginative retelling of an Athabascan legend by Native American author Velma Wallis. The story begins with a tribe under threat of starvation, and the two women of the title have become two more hungry mouths to feed. Unfortunately, they are complainers, not contributors, and the tribe sadly but firmly leaves them behind when it's time to move camp. With winter coming, this means the two women will surely die.

There's nothing unbelievable about the anger and denial the women feel, nothing fantastical or magical about what their ordeal brings forth in them—courage, integrity, strength and hard-earned survival skills, along with reservoirs of character and heart. When the tribe returns and finds them, everyone's assumptions of what's possible in old age is expanded, including the assumptions of the two women themselves.

The experience of reading the story reminded me of the day Bernice handed me a copy of *Little Women* in the children's library when I was twelve. That book had also almost perfectly addressed a transition I was experiencing, and I'd felt relief. Now, in old age, *Two Old Women* affirmed my knowledge of aging, including the pains, doubts, and complaints as well as the ways I've pushed through and gotten stronger. The story gave me something to hold on to, to remember the whole of my experience, not only the difficulties. Here again was solid literary ground to stand on and the vision of something not only to recognize, but to keep reaching for within myself.

Stories help us clear the space around us, clear our heads, clear the way. A good story can—as *Two Old Women* did for me that day when I ached and dreaded the change in seasons—help to prepare a person for winter.

PART THREE

Weathering

The Ages of Grief

A couple of years after my brother Bruce died by suicide at nineteen, we moved from Minnesota to South Dakota, but my parents still read the *Minneapolis Star and Tribune* each morning, its wide pages passed along to me by my father as he finished them. When the obituaries came around, I ignored most unless a teenager had died in some tragic way—a car accident, a fall from a cliff, a gas station robbery, or especially by suicide.

Bruce was almost seven years older than me. He was brilliant, funny, and had lots of friends. He gave movie reviews at the dinner table that made me laugh, even if I'd liked the movie and his take oozed with disdain. When he was a junior in high school, he put a streak of orange in his curly black hair with peroxide, making him the one and only punk in the tiny town of Pipestone, Minnesota, and that was 1955. He was the only other family member with a matching passion for literature. Like me, he'd spent his earliest years on our librarian aunt's lap, turning the pages of picture books. Ever since then, he'd read constantly and sometimes recommended books to me.

I devoured each one of the obituaries about kids dying tragically. I studied the young faces in the photographs and tried to imagine what their lives had been like and what they would have turned into as time passed and they'd had the chance to grow up. What would the lives of their families look like in the years to come—heartbroken and emotionally adrift like ours had been since Bruce's death, and even more so now, after my brother Michael's departure from home shortly afterward so that he, only a teenager himself, could join the Navy? Or would these perhaps wiser siblings and parents bounce back in some admirable way I could only struggle to imagine? I sometimes wished I could talk to those families. I wondered what I could learn from them.

Grief, that useful umbrella term for a bundle of emotions—shock, sadness, longing, regret, anger, loneliness, confusion, guilt—was not a topic, not in midwestern life anyway, at the time. You didn't find understanding descriptions of what to expect after a death and what to do about it in the Health or Living sections of the newspaper in the early 1960s. For that matter, you didn't find Health or Living sections. Millions of us grew up with no guideposts, including my parents before me and all previous generations.

My parents never used the word *grief* and stayed mostly quiet about Bruce. My sister, Marla, seven years younger than me, had severe mental disabilities and was the one most likely to bring up his absence. "Where's Boo?" she might ask out of the blue, and we, a nonreligious family, would try to think of a way to answer her. No matter what we said, the question would pop up again later. Nothing satisfied her, and she was right to be unsatisfied. I hid my grief from my parents, afraid to upset them more than they were already, but Marla freely expressed her sadness. He was gone. It was inexplicable. She felt that the subject—at least for as long as it took her to give up on our providing any reliable answers—should not be closed.

In those early mornings at the kitchen table with the newspaper, I paid little attention to the deaths of anyone who had been fifty, sixty, or older and had died in what I considered a normal way, a sickness. My eyes glazed over their photographs. Those people were really old. They had not much time left anyway. I might, or more likely might not, have felt a stir of sadness for their families before I put the paper down. But then I was a kid, soon heading out the door to school. Weren't they expecting it, after all, these older people? Those deaths were not tragedies but natural occurrences. At that time, Bruce's death was the only one I knew, and consequently the only one that felt real, and it felt horrible.

It didn't occur to me that anyone would be hurting greatly over the loss of the people whose obituaries I spent no time on. It would take getting old myself to learn the variety of wrappings the sorrows of the old come in: the deaths of mothers, fathers, siblings, cousins, aunts, and uncles, friends, neighbors, doctors, familiar store clerks and bus drivers and long-time mail deliverers. Unless we're Buddhist monks or completely oblivious, we're subject to spells of grief and reactivated grief, long or short, for those who depart this earth at any time for any reason.

Of four children, I am now the last one living. Marla, my tender-hearted, forthright, honest-to-the-bone, prankster sister—the only sibling who called my parents by their first names, Roger and Alice, all her life, always treating them utterly as equals—died long ago in an institution at the age of twenty-seven. Michael, my beautiful, guitar-playing, pun-making, crossword-puzzle-whiz brother, died of cancer at sixty-three. My parents have also both died.

It may no longer be news to me that death is real and around us all the time, but it's always a surprise to find that it feels real in a new way each time someone I've known dies. Sallie Tisdale writes in *Advice for Future Corpses (and Those Who Love Them): A Practical*

Perspective on Death and Dying: "We walk around with a blinkered, partial denial of death. Yes, we will die, but not now, not here. This dissonance is strong and strange—to absolutely know this will happen, and against all evidence to the contrary, to absolutely not know." The dissonance applies not only to ourselves but stretches out to encompass those we know and love and those we have known and loved.

Quite recently, someone I'd been friends with many years ago died of complications from diabetes. Back in the 1970s, Diane had been a hippie mama. She wore tie-dye, let her body grow large and round, cooked only vegetarian meals for her kids, let them make up their own minds about religion and politics, and started a non-profit for teenagers in need. Our paths diverged, but we kept friends in common. When I learned of her death, naturally my mind wandered back to the years we'd known each other well. I also noticed that my first reaction had been: *But she's only seventy-four.*

How could I think that dying in our seventies is dying too soon? The only possible route this thought could have taken was if it had leaped over my understanding of how a lifespan works and all of my own life experience, including my knowledge of the possibility of sudden death from the age of thirteen on. Yet, there it was.

Unless we are actually sitting in a hospice room with someone we've known for many years and are present for their process of dying, it seems that death always has the power to knock us sideways, at least for a while. We grieve. If we are lucky, each time we learn of the death of someone who meant something to us, either now or long ago, the understanding and love of friends and family helps us through. So frequent is the sideways knocking of the old as the deaths mount up that to expect some sort of brave face from them all the time amounts to cruelty. No matter how many years we've lived, grief needs to be a topic of conversation: *Your friend died, your sister died, your last remaining uncle died. Please tell me about your friend, your sister, your uncle.*

My young self would have probably thought paying this kind of attention to those old people who had known the newly dead old people was odd. Unless gifted with compassion and sensitivity, which of course some are, the average adolescent might suppose that after a certain age people expect and accept not only the loss of people they love but the imminent loss of their very own lives, that is, *all they are and know*, along with departure from a planet that's been home for over sixty, seventy, eighty, ninety years. I didn't understand in my youth that acceptance is a practice, not something you receive as a by-product of aging.

Even though she longed to talk to others so very much, my teenage self had, by example, been given to understand that conversation wasn't necessary, just like all the other millions of people, now in their sixties and seventies and older, who grew up under the same belief system. If we bought into it, we are now expected to be ready to go and to be ready, somehow, for our friends and other beloved people to go, without putting up much of a fuss. The truth of the matter is that, for those of us in this age range, death is welcome only when it relieves suffering. Otherwise, we, like everyone else, would like it to take a step back, please. Maybe more than a step.

Deaths are not the only events mourned at this time of life. There are many sorts of grieving we know: the loss of camaraderie and conversation with friends and relatives who suffer from dementia, Alzheimer's disease, or significant hearing loss; the loss of dear friendships through misunderstandings, which can happen at any age of course, but is particularly painful after fifty years or so of a friendship; the alienation from younger relatives we love due to drug addiction or alcoholism or, in some cases, political divides; pink slips delivered to our desks at jobs we thought we'd keep until retirement; homes we've lived in for decades lost through natural disaster or bankruptcy or the fact we cannot keep them in good repair; drivers' licenses revoked due to infirmity; and of course the body itself breaking down and losing one capacity or another, bit by bit or all by all. The real wonder of it, a wise young person might consider, is that a good portion of the old aren't mowed down by grief alone. Sometimes they are, even though a medical report lists other causes.

We see things from where we are. These days when I open a newspaper (or most likely an online news site) and read about the death of anyone at any age, I think about the people who loved them, and I have more than a glimmer as to how those left behind might be feeling. One of the many wonders of these later years is what happens when I encounter sad, perhaps devastating, events in the news. My mind sweeps over its knowledge of such things, whether personal or through friendships, like a breeze passing over a variety of prairie grasses: big bluestem, salt grass, bottlebrush, porcupine, timothy, cup grass, tufted lovegrass, wild rye. It is asking, *Which one is this*? And then comes a moment when a known grief springs up green and fresh. *Oh yes, this kind again.*

One real advantage of old age is that you know the strength of grief. You know that, after the heavy sobbing is over, after you think you've finally gotten a grip, a casual remark by a neighbor, a comment by a newscaster, the fragrance of a perfume that wafts past you as you walk down the street, the sighting of a certain flower, or the mention of a place—any of these can suddenly knock you off balance and into tears and longing again. So you know what a powerful force grief is; you have learned to expect it to be powerful.

Another significant advantage is that you also know how grief works in *your* psyche specifically. I know, for example, that in the event of any death of someone near to me, my mind will tug hard on the string that brings up all the deceased and beloved family members and friends and their absence from Bruce on. That's how it is with me, and I accept it. I also know I will listen to music a lot more than usual, and I'll play it loud. It doesn't even matter what it is, as long as it's something that helps me to feel. I will put aside whatever novel I'm reading and turn to Emily Dickinson and other poets. I'll be sleepless for a while, and when I begin to fall asleep easily again, I'll instruct myself to dream of the missing one, to at least make contact in the unconscious if I can't have them in waking life.

A good friend of mine, Leslie, a musician, died eight years ago this coming summer. Her artist husband, Bill, completely lost, decided to take himself into his studio every day and paint and then share his work in a blog, and he decided to say yes to all invitations extended to him. These were exactly the right things for Bill to do. He began to steadily build a new body of work and contact with other painters, and he stayed in touch and in the presence of those who loved him.

Saying *yes* and going out and away from the house Bill and Leslie shared together for many years didn't end my friend's grief—he still feels Leslie's absence keenly even now—but it did link him back to life, which he did not want to leave, regardless of how much pain he was in. Even though I may not say yes to all invitations when I'm grieving, I learned from him. I know I won't want to go out and see anyone, and I know it's important to do it sometimes anyway because it always gives me something new to think about. I don't want to give up thinking about my friend or relative who died, not at all, but I want to continue to be open to new thoughts, new events, life.

I know that, eventually, I'll also look for those books that bring my friend or relative or neighbor, whomever I've lost, back to me. This particular piece of coping I learned from Bruce, who dropped a breadcrumb for me all those years ago.

By the time I sat at that kitchen table with my father and the newspaper, I'd already read the last book that Bruce had strongly recommended to me, *Wuthering Heights*. I knew it held something important because of the way he'd talked about how I *needed* to read it, but I didn't know what to look for. At first I thought he'd wanted me to try to imagine my way into the feelings of a thwarted romance, something he'd also experienced, but as I've reread it several times over the years, I've come to understand it wasn't the love story that he felt so deeply and wanted me to see. It's Emily Brontë's description of a tortured soul who cannot even begin to deal with powerful emotions in any sort of constructive way and is overwhelmed and undone by them. The part of my brother I couldn't have known once upon a time becomes visible whenever I read this novel, and I keep company with him in those pages.

I know this about my own version of grief, too: I will talk to friends. I'll talk and talk and talk. Fortunately, I've made friends along the way who have either known hardships and loss themselves, some of them far exceeding my own, or are gifted with a compassion I sensed in our earliest conversations. As I grew up, I cultivated relationships with wise, insightful, and perceptive people, and I asked these people questions and sought advice. A few times I've consulted therapists and paid for guidance. It was worth it.

Once I was an adult and realized that everybody suffers and many actually can articulate how they've lived with their suffering, I began to find wisdom almost everywhere. I read novels and nonfiction that embraced hard subjects, especially death and dying. And I've tried to allow compassion, love, and creativity to help me move forward. I've used all of these things and continue to use them when faced with grief. I've not become an expert on the subject, but I have learned I can depend on myself to find help and especially to seek out, to actually ask for what Marla had asked for: the chance to talk about hard things and let love and understanding in.

I wish I could speak to that young girl sitting at the breakfast table in South Dakota searching the newspaper for some experience like her own, looking for answers about how to proceed with her life. I'd comfort her and tell her that one day not far off she'd move away from the prairie to a different part of the country, but even there, like the peaks of happiness that would eventually come into view, losses would always be part of the landscape, too. They might come at different ages and in as many forms as prairie grass, a fact of life, but the older we become, the more we carry within us to meet each one.

Weathering

One January morning not long ago, the body of a woman in her sixties was found floating in the river several yards from my door. She was discovered by two men who had been working for several hours on righting my houseboat, which had started to tip dangerously to one side under the weight of an unusually heavy snowfall in Portland, another in an almost unheard-of series. The men set out and as their tugboat skirted the breakwater, a string of logs that prevents wakes from damaging the houseboats, they came upon the body.

I knew nothing of the discovery until I came home after running errands and saw police cars in our parking lot. I'd been grateful that morning to escape the houseboat because the latest blizzard had prevented me from getting out for supplies or distraction for many days. The hill leading from the moorage to the highway had only that day become passable. As I unloaded groceries from the car, a neighbor walked over to tell me what had happened. The deceased woman was clothed and "looked normal," he said. By this I understood her death had happened recently and there were no signs of foul play.

My thoughts turned to a recent article I'd read about Multnomah County's River Patrol. They reported that thirty to fifty bodies are found in the water every year. Given boating, alcohol, drugs, and plain ignorance of the power of our two rivers, the Columbia and the Willamette, many people die in accidents. Given a dozen bridges and the fact that suicide is often a matter of convenience in terms of method, many die by jumping. Because of the time of year and the recent terrible weather, I suspected this woman's death was probably not due to a boating accident.

During January I think more intensely about suicide than I do the rest of the year, although it's a subject always close at hand— not a contemplation of my own suicide but my brother's, which happened on New Year's night over sixty years ago. Bruce was also born in January, and he was nineteen when he died by gun-shot in the basement of our house while the rest of us were away visiting relatives for the holidays. He'd stayed behind to work and to see friends back from college for the holidays and, we learned later, to propose to a new girlfriend. She had turned him down on the night he died.

Bruce's depression was deep, noted more by friends, we discovered after his death, than by us, his family. I was thirteen, and I'd thought my brother had become sullen and touchy for some unknowable reason. Mental illness was something no one talked about in our small community. If you felt unable to cope, you were supposed to snap out of it. My brother's illness, nevertheless, was real and had been aggravated by several things: a breakup early in the fall with another young woman, his high school sweet-heart, who went off to college in Iowa; the departure of the rest of his family for North Dakota to be with my grandmother for the holidays; a job driving a delivery truck when he longed to be in college himself but had no money to attend; the harsh Minnesota winter; frustration about a future within a town so small one could 'circle the square," as we called the four streets enclosing businesses, churches, and houses, in less than fifteen minutes. I sometimes picture him in that town on that bitterly cold night, a new year beginning but nothing to look forward to, all of us away, anguish overwhelming him, his gun in the basement, the irresistible impulse to go down and grab it, the inability to even climb the stairs again, drink some coffee, think about options. He died only a few feet from where he kept the gun.

And so the month of January frames my older brother, as well as others in my family who were born and/or died in that month. I think of Bruce often, but in January I invite him to come live more fully, more daily, in my heart so that I might once again come to terms with the fact that he's missing and I miss him.

I was in this annual mental state when the woman was found. Each time I hear of someone dying by suicide, which appeared likely in her case, I feel a little mental earthquake as old pain and misery are shaken from the rafters. A kind of emotional dust drifts down and blankets my thoughts. Maybe anyone who has lost a loved one in a tornado or a plane crash is reminded of their loss when hearing about similar catastrophes in the news. A thread of grief connects us to the new event, and we might dwell there a bit longer than others in the population who haven't experienced anything similar. Few of my neighbors mentioned this woman at all, for example, after the police left that day. If the subject came up, they quickly moved on to other topics. I didn't feel I was being morbid, as they might have felt about me, had we talked about her for as long as I actually wanted to talk about her. I felt only that I had a stake in the experience they didn't have.

I learned the woman was in her late sixties—only a few years younger than I. I recalled that it's in our sixties when most of us who have previously been fortunate enough to live in good health begin to feel the first perplexing inklings of vulnerability. If she died because she'd wanted to die, I tried to imagine what might have caused her to make her way to the river. The older we get, the higher the odds of life tipping over: isolation, sickness, chronic pain, unexpected or steadily increasing poverty, the deaths of friends, side effects of new meds, mix-ups in old meds, loss of a partner, a beloved animal companion, a home, or a neighbor on whom we've counted for many years. One or more of these things could have beset the life of this person. There's a high rate of suicide among the middle-aged and older, and it is now the twelfth leading cause of death in the United States, according to the National Institute of Mental Health.

It also seemed quite possible that the harshness of our winter added strains that older people feel more keenly. Usually it snows on average four days a year in Portland, but we'd been hit that winter by five extended winter storms between early December and mid-January. For that long spell, heavy and then heavier snow had muffled our normally drippy, puddly, splashy environment. White robes hid the lively green of the thousands of trees around us. When freezing rain encased the snow, branches snapped and tumbled from great firry heights, plopping onto power lines, shutting down heat and lights. City roads were neither salted nor graveled. Skittering into a ditch became, more and more, a real possibility.

A normal winter can be hard on a houseboat dweller, thanks to rain falling daily from gray skies onto a gray-green river that swells with the increase in water along with snow melt from the mountains, threatening floods. I'd already lived through two winters,

1996 and 1997, when the river rose so high the dock to which the houseboats are attached nearly floated up and over the pilings that hold it in place, which would have meant our whole moorage could have been set adrift in a fast current.

For days on end, during that winter when the woman's body was found, snow fell relentlessly. My anxiety increased as this beautiful wonderland became claustrophobic. With storms of any kind, the stresses on houseboats increase—a houseboat is a house on water, after all, and there are some circumstances where, even if you can leave, it isn't wise to jump ship and leave your home's fate to nature. We'd been forced inside. Our cars sat still as frightened rabbits in the vast parking lot at the edge of the forest.

I read, made a lot of soup, listened to music, and continued to work until the power went off. Since I have only electric heat, I went next door for a couple of nights to play cribbage with neighbors by lantern light beside their woodstove, warming up enough to come home and crawl under a heap of blankets with my cat.

Even the otter family, regular chirruping rollickers on the riverbank outside my back door, wriggled up the hill and into the woods, darting back down again only for a quick fish hunt. On their hunts they could have observed the dangerous tipping of my house. They could have watched through the windows as my neighbor Julia helped me move furniture from the side of the house almost touching the river to the other side for ballast, and as neighbors John and Morgan brought ropes and chains to tie up tighter to the dock and keep the house from sinking, an increasingly real threat.

I continually swept new snow from my decks. Other neighbors and I used long-handled rakes to get at least some of its dreaded weight off our houses; a few people even climbed onto the roofs of a neighboring houseboat to try to reach across to the roof next door and drag the snow downward and into the river.

After these efforts, if the otters peered through the windows, they'd have spotted me anxiously pacing in my tippy house in the dying light of day, bundled in sweaters and jacket, arms wrapped around myself. No lights. No heat. Furniture piled on furniture.

Weather forecasters warned that more snow lurked in the flat gray skies, but they didn't talk about how to weather the weather, about depression or feeling cut off from others or how to cope with the possibility of a mind treading water, a houseboat sinking.

Later, after the storm ended and the woman's body was found, I wondered if snow had been falling on the day she'd departed from her regular life, falling steadily, accompanying her and silencing everything around her as she walked. I thought of Conrad Aiken's short story, "Silent Snow, Secret Snow," in which a boy loses his mind to a dream world of snow.

On winter nights back in the Midwest, the elders in my family, as in many families, used to tell stories about what they called "real cold." They talked about how farmers, even during blizzards, needed to go to the barn to milk the cows and would sometimes lose their internal compass in the white swirl on their way back to the farmhouse. They would finally give up and fall asleep, which meant the end. When the blizzard died away, they'd be found curled around themselves in the farmyard. Before cars or telephones, the old ones said to us, roaring winds and weeks of snowfall would drive otherwise stable men and women into what was called "prairie fever." Many succumbed because they'd been city dwellers from the east or came from small towns to try to make a living from a land with no trees to break the wind and no neighbors for miles. They weren't experiencing what we now call cabin fever, a light dose of boredom, but an agitated, excruciatingly lonely and anxious state of mind that they couldn't "snap out of," and sometimes it drove them to open the farmhouse door and walk out farther and farther into the enemy itself, winter, until they disappeared.

My midwestern relatives would have considered Portland's weather, even with its recent severity, as troublesome yet relatively mild, but because it was so unexpected and because the unexpected lasted so long, it created a feeling of unreality for some of us who have lived here a long time. Housebound, cut off from normal routines, some may have thrived, but many of us felt embattled, restless.

How had the woman found floating in the river been weathering this strange winter? Had at least some of her thinking been affected by the cold? Our brains, too, feel the cold. They get sluggish and stupefied and capable of turning down the wrong dark, internal lanes. Snow loses its beauty and becomes menacing. Had she, like those farmers cooped up to the point of insanity many years ago, walked out her front door and straight into the arms of the enemy defiant or broken? How long had her body floated in those near freezing waters? Was she missed by anyone? I hoped she was missed. I did not want to think of her as a woman whose absence would be noted but not mourned. In time, I did not want to think too much more about her at all because it made me feel much sadder than I already was, and I had to concentrate on keeping my house afloat for the rest of the season and beyond.

Sometime in February after the storms were finished with us, I spoke with the wife of the diver who had come to my houseboat to save it from its dangerous tilting by placing additional flotation underneath. We needed to settle up our bill, but we talked easily about other things, and our conversation that day soon led to the woman her husband and his partner had found after their tugboat pulled away from my house. She told me that the partner, in his seventies, had quit that very day. He wanted no more of what these Oregon rivers might put in his way.

I sympathized. After their discovery, the inclement weather, and the normal January sorrow I'd been feeling—and after noticing that it was becoming harder for me to shovel snow away from my own small section of the walkway—life on the river hadn't looked the same to me either. For a while, I thought seriously of moving elsewhere.

Then spring came. The winter had been awful, but the sight of raptors in flight outside my window, the departure of the dozens of silent black cormorants that sit on the pilings outside the houseboats from October to May, the return of vocal red-winged blackbirds in the jewelweed covering the logs of the breakwater, and the birth of otter pups on the riverbank all reminded me of the privilege it is to live here. I couldn't leave this place. Not yet.

As spring settled in and swept winter aside and my heart lightened as hearts do when that finally happens, I found myself thinking again about the woman who had drowned. With the sun shining and my house secure, with the blackbirds hopping around my deck happily gobbling up birdseed and the otter pups peeping in the weeds along the backwater, I could try to find out more about who she was without sinking into despair myself.

I found her memorial page and learned she'd been challenged by health issues. I read comments addressed to her from several friends. From these I gleaned she loved the earth, participated wholeheartedly in any group she was part of, and would be greatly missed. No one mentioned suicide, but they didn't cite another cause of death either.

I looked at her photograph. Her pale skin contrasted with a simple, darkly patterned dress. She had a gentle look, white hair, and the kind of ease in her face that comes with loving and being loved. She looked like a woman I'd have smiled at if we'd passed each other in the aisle of a grocery store or on the street. I felt better that I knew more about her through the memorial tributes.

I felt close to her in a way, too. We'd been two women in trouble one stormy winter. We'd both been challenged, though in different ways. I could have lost my house to the river. One more heavy snowfall followed by freezing rain and the weight would have pushed the southeast corner of it down into the water, and that would have been followed by a slow but probably irreversible submersion. She'd fought an even more serious battle, trying to stay alive through medical intervention and then, because of medications or depression or both, and perhaps the weather, too, she'd let go.

I've known how it feels to be a survivor for quite a while. It's been a long spell now since my brother's death. Many of us who have experienced a sudden and shocking loss by suicide can feel that life ought to be lived more fully because part of you lives for the one who felt unable to carry on. Bruce stopped his life when he was barely on the cusp of manhood. He knew nothing much at all of life's possibilities. His death came too soon.

But *too soon* doesn't apply when I contemplate the death of the woman found in the river. Each of us weathers these later years differently. The memorial page gave no details of her troubles, her physical pain or discomforts, the dangerous curves a mix of medications can throw at a body and mind, the toll of long-term illness on a spirit. All I can know is that she'd had lots of life experience, and she knew by this time of her life what death would mean, how final.

As for me, so far I am too curious about old age and all it brings to want to leave it. I feel fortunate to have friends, work, this spot on the planet. I'm aware things can tip, that the weight of continuing can bear down at a moment's notice. I take nothing for granted anymore. I listen and watch with keener interest than ever. It seems to me that this is how I should have been living all along. But it's not too late.

Meanwhile, I carry the woman who died in this river with me. She's not a burden. This coming January I'll light a candle for her and for Bruce and others lost, and one for the river beneath me and outside my door, too, because the river holds so much power, so much life, even the lives of some who can't bear any more to hold fast to their own.

Before Your Eyes

Time is being and being
time, it is all one thing,
the shining, the seeing,
the dark abounding.
—URSULA K. LE GUIN, FROM *LATE IN THE DAY*

I slipped the watch from my father's bruised and punctured arm. Keeping track of time had been important to him. He'd never been late for anything in his life. Now, no more hours, no more minutes, no more chances to be on time.

My mother had called me the previous afternoon. It was February and cold, Iowa winter cold. I'd sped in a rental car from the Des Moines airport thirty miles north to Ames. It was almost midnight when I pulled into the hospital parking lot. My fingers trembled as I switched off the ignition. I got out of the car and hurried toward the building that seemed both too far away and too close. Head bowed against a slicing wind, hands deep in my pockets, I crossed a wide driveway.

My watering eyes caught the mouse at first only as a blur of movement. Then he took shape in a rectangle of light pouring from a window. Tiny and covered in the thinnest of fur coats, he stopped and hesitated a few seconds before zipping across the concrete driveway toward the parking lot. I thought that driveway must have seemed as wide as the Atlantic Ocean to a little being like him, and he was going entirely in the wrong direction. What he needed was a clump of grass, a hole, a fallen bough— any warmth the frozen earth could offer. My heart felt shredded with agony for him, for my father, for myself, for everything in the world.

I walked down a dim corridor that led to the room and the bed where my father lay dying. My mother stood beside him. She was eighty-five; he was eighty-two. He hadn't opened his eyes for a couple of days, she said. But then she leaned over to tell him I was there, and his eyelids fluttered open for a few seconds, long enough to see me before they closed again. I felt helpless to do anything but repeat what she'd told him. "Dad," I said. "I'm here."

He was on oxygen and in some awful contraption, a white bandage-like thing tied over and around his head and strapped under his chin. A life-long smoker, he was dying of emphysema. I had no idea what this white thing was for. It was part of all the awfulness, part of the beige room with machines flashing, buzzing and beeping, part of the sight of my mother standing as close as she could get to the bed, anguish in her face. The white sling under his chin made no more sense than any of this, and I did not ask about it.

He hadn't wanted to come to the hospital. My mother had wanted it, and I'd also encouraged him to go when we talked on the phone the week before. I'd hoped they could make him comfortable and give him something to help him get back to his own bed, his own chair, his nature and history shows, the magazines he liked to read, his small comforts. But there was nothing here for him except the beeping and the contraption and the flashing lights.

My mother had told me that he'd been in this bed several days before he'd asked a nurse when he was going home, and she'd replied, "Oh, you. You're not going home." Stunned, he'd reported this to my mother when she'd come to his room later. She could barely grasp either the reality of it or the cruelty. Hearing all that had been bad enough, but seeing him lying there, I felt terrible. I should never have suggested he come to this place.

I moved to the other side of the bed to stand next to my brother, Michael, my only surviving sibling, two years older than I at fifty-eight. We hugged but said nothing, only stood close. Two or three times a phlebotomist came in to draw blood, but each one had a difficult time finding a vein because they were all soft by then, the whole flower of this once so handsome, athletic, funny, and difficult man wilting. Each frustrated person would give up. Each explained they needed to go find someone with more experience who could come and take another stab, a literal stab, at the black and blue arms.

I felt dazed to see my father's thin body looking small under a sheet, broken-hearted by my mother and brother's stoic silence. I lived far away and had not seen my family for several months. My mind buzzed and beeped like one of the machines. Not a single coherent thought came to me.

I came out of my shock long enough to ask the next phlebotomist who walked through the door why they kept doing this, poking my father. What was their reasoning? He shook his head, said he would go talk to someone, and after that the repeated wounding of the arms ended. Yet now those arms could not stop moving. They rose and fell, jerked and settled, rose again.

Nurses came in and out, shutting off overhead lights, adjusting things. The early morning hours rolled in. One or two asked if we wanted them to give my father morphine, but that's all they said. *Do you want morphine?*

Michael and I hadn't ever been around a dying person before, and our mother, Alice, had never been at anyone's bedside for their last hours in a hospital during modern times. Nobody told us what morphine would do, how it could help. We could barely hear them ask anyway because we were too much inside of what we were losing. They came and went all the time for this machine or that, or to change fluids in a bag hanging above the bed. It was nearly three in the morning before one of us actually heard this question about morphine and thought to ask more about it. As soon as we understood it, we agreed to it. The strange movements of my father's arms stopped shortly after the nurse injected him. Why no one explained morphine earlier, I don't know. Maybe the doctor had told my mother about it, but if so, she hadn't understood him.

My brother and I took turns sleeping in an uncomfortable chair in a nearby room. All night long my mother stood next to the bed, refusing to sit. Later, she would ask why none of us had talked to my father throughout that long night. I couldn't answer. I'd had a lifelong love and fear of him. Would he come home from work gentle and full of wit, or would he snap at us? Or would he not come home until long after we were in bed? If we did happen to be awake, would he be dismissive and mean, possibly raging after a night of drinking? Would he threaten to give us something to cry about when we cried over things he'd said that had hurt us, or would he offer comfort? We who were the older three children might get a long and angry stare across the dinner table had any of us misbehaved while he'd been at work. Marla was never punished, never the recipient of any negativity from him.

Michael, my mother, and I stayed with my father now, watching over him, distant from our childhoods, far away from the tumultuous earlier years of the marriage. He'd threatened to leave but never left. In fact, he'd settled down. So we'd both loved and feared him. I didn't know how to say any of this in this place and at the end.

We may not have spoken much that night, but we did touch my father. I had never before felt so free to touch him. We rubbed his legs, his feet, his hands, and his arm that hadn't been stabbed with needles as many times. The horrible contraption around his head—what was it and why didn't I ask?—made it impossible to touch his face, but if we could have, we would have done that, too.

On went the night with its fitful sleeps in the chair, my mother refusing to sit, the nurses coming and going, in and out, in and out of the darkened room. Time as we knew it had abandoned us and *now* was black windows, the hum of a wallboard heater, distant buzzers, nurses' voices.

By the time my nephew came through the door the next morning, the three of us were tucked into the bosom of death where only our closeness to one another mattered, and we drew him in with us. So there we stood surrounding my father's bed, and there he lay with that terrible thing around his head and not one of us thought to make them take it off because we were under the spell of the strange rules of hospitals that can overcome common sense.

My father's breathing slowed. A little after 9 a.m., he died. Michael stood on one side of the bed, I on the other. At the moment of death, our eyes met. It had been a rough ride for all of us with this man, but yes, we loved him, and we all cried.

Soon a nurse came in and gently urged us to leave. We drifted out the door, one by one. I was the last to go, but I didn't get very far. Almost as soon as the door closed behind me, I turned around and went alone back into his room.

He'd been proud of the watch that now lay on his still arm, ticking softly. Once he'd been a poor kid on a ranch that was seized by the bank during the Depression, but he'd made it out of poverty on his terms, landing in his old age financially far enough from where he'd started so that he could mostly stop worrying about money, at least not all the time. He'd succeeded in other ways, too, as a human being. We'd been good for him in that way, this family that he originally didn't want but had finally made peace with having, forgetting at last about the pressure put on him by his parents to marry the girl he'd gotten pregnant and to have a family, our family. We'd softened him over the years, made him care about something beyond himself, and in return he'd taken care of us.

To honor all of that—and put aside the years of difficulty he'd caused us—I wanted to wear the watch, even though it was too big. It would be a way to carry him with me for a while, and anyway, I wasn't ready yet to leave him all alone in that hospital room.

I'd wanted a keepsake. I wasn't expecting anything more, but my father had always taught me things I couldn't learn anywhere else, starting when I was nine and he told me to stop believing everything my teachers told me about history. George Washington wasn't a pure and honest man, he'd said, to my amazement. He told me about slavery. He told me about poverty, about real people needing help that other people could give but sometimes, often in fact, refused to give. He rigorously questioned the government's choices, regardless of which party was in power. To his last days, he'd subscribed to *Mother Jones* and the *Nation*. He was his progressive, suffragette mother's son.

He knew some of the truths he told me were hard lessons, but he gave them to me anyway, and I'm grateful for that. He taught me, too, about nature. On each winter solstice he'd take me to the window as the sun went down and say, "Every day from now on will be a hen step longer." He loved animals. He would have cared about the mouse racing across the hospital driveway in the freezing cold, heading in the wrong direction.

And so I would, I decided, take a piece of his life with me. I walked over to the bed and gently eased the watch over his fingers and put it on my wrist. The moment I did this, I happened to look into his face. Instead of being completely empty of life as it had been only moments before, it was as if the bandage, death, and time itself fell away, replaced at first by the soft features of a small child, followed by the face of a serious and struggling little boy, a thin and hungry ranch kid, and then sharpening into adolescence, a young man, and very quickly transforming into a mature man, an older man, an old man.

Your life passes in a flash before your eyes when you die. How many times had I heard this? I didn't know why it was happening now, with only the two of us, but I understood, as I stood so close to him, that I'd been his mirror. He'd always looked more to me than his other children to reflect his interests: people, politics, books, community, friends. I knew somehow that what had just happened occurred because of the watch, moving it from his wrist to mine. As he passed, he passed time itself to me.

Sometimes I look back on this experience and hardly believe it happened, but then I remember those faces passing by. It's hard to describe how clear each of them was and yet how quickly they came and went. Who wants to believe that we're here for such a brief moment it can all be seen in a mere flash, like a comet shooting through space, then dying out? As for me, that moment or whatever it was—whether it had been in or outside of time, I didn't know—put me completely in touch with the whole of my father, the whole of his life. I stopped being his mirror and became his witness to the shining, the seeing, the dark abounding.

When We Were Two

My mother and I stood in line behind the third oldish-daughter-with-old-mother unit I'd seen since entering the grocery store. The mother ahead of us was tall, late eighties, thin and weak looking but sharp-eyed. She turned to give appraising glances at the weary, preoccupied string of humanity behind her. After she'd summed us up, she leaned forward and rested her arms on the shopping cart.

The daughter was in her sixties, as I was at the time. She had a long frame like her mother's but fleshed out and smartly dressed. She stared at a row of magazine covers showing movie stars wearing dresses split to their waists. The V-shaped bodices gave peeka-boo glimpses of youthful, swelling breasts: America's fertility goddesses bedecked in designer gowns and diamonds.

These mother/daughter sets I'd started to spot everywhere couldn't be new, I thought. I'd probably never seen them because I wasn't paying attention. But that summer my life had changed. I'd become the younger half of such a unit myself when my mother moved from Iowa to Oregon to live in an assisted living facility near me.

Alice missed her quiet Iowa life. Whenever we left the residence for a medical appointment or a shopping trip, she objected to the size of Portland on principle. Did a town need to be so big, so spread out? She especially missed the house she'd lived in for over forty years. She wasn't comfortable eating with strangers or passing them in hallways or having aides come into her space at all hours to see if she was okay. She depended heavily on me to bring the familiar, that is, my very self, into her new life, and so I spent an hour or two at her apartment daily, often longer.

Whereas before she'd called me or I'd called her perhaps once or twice a week, she now called me four or more times a day. I was trying to get used to these interruptions, chalking them up to her anxiety, which I hoped would diminish as she got more comfortable with her surroundings. In the meantime, I felt grateful for her sense of humor, her daily supply of anecdotes about her fellow "inmates," as she called them, the way she nicknamed those whose real names she didn't know. Mr. Fickle was the resident male flirt; a raven-haired woman in her seventies, whom she called The Young and the Restless, was the female version.

Adjustment for both of us was proving challenging, but she'd always liked shopping, and that day we had spent an hour in the store. In the checkout line, she was patient and in good humor. She put up with the long grocery line and used our cart as a walker to move forward. As we got closer to the register, she leaned sideways to squint at the glossy magazines and asked in a loud voice, "What are those girls wearing? Are they supposed to be dresses?"

The other mother turned her head and took in the booby view. "They must have run out of material," she said.

An old joke, but I felt glad for a laugh. Alice, with her poor hearing, missed it. She turned to me, questioning. I repeated the woman's remark and she smiled at the other mother.

I tried to make eye contact with the daughter, but she glanced toward the door, perhaps thinking about getting home. To whom, I wondered. Was someone waiting? Did she live with her mother? Or alone? What would she do after dinner that night? Read? Pour a glass of wine and watch something on Netflix? Call a friend and go over her day? Fall asleep wishing for a carefree life again?

I wanted to know about other daughters. How were they holding up? Being a new caregiver had altered my days dramatically. I could barely keep up with the to-do lists, errands, medical scheduling, and the financial stress. With Alice in my life, even at an assisted living facility, the demands on my time were so great that I could no longer hold down a job. I was paying for my day-to-day expenses from my savings account and struggling with the enormous change from a life filled with lots of time for reading, writing, and friends to a whole lot of Alice time. Yet, I felt a fresh sense of purpose in caregiving, and so far that had felt good.

When the daughter ahead of us finally did turn our way, her face looked strained. She glanced peevishly at her mother and moved a few inches away from her. I knew then that I didn't ever want to feel about my mother the way she did about hers in that moment. She appeared tired of comments meant to be funny and bored by impromptu connections with strangers. Given a contentious history, I knew Alice and I could land in that place, but I vowed to try to find the grace not to let it happen. My mother was ninety-four, after all. How much time did we have left, anyway?

I wasn't yet aware of the emotional, mental, and physical hazards of caregiving, so I had no context for understanding that daughter's look and behavior. I didn't yet know that 91 percent of the people caring for women elders are daughters, and these daughters spend twice as much time caregiving as sons do. Many lose thousands of dollars a year from their jobs due to time spent away from work for caregiving. They're prone to stress-related health problems and experience more depression and anxiety than the rest of the population.

Minority and low-income women suffer the most because 30 to 40 percent of single older women in these groups hit poverty levels. According to the Family Caregiver Alliance, these women are "half as likely as higher-income caregivers to have paid home health care or assistance available to provide support for and relief from their caregiving functions."

Alice's anxiety about her new circumstances did eventually decrease. She settled into her new home, and, because she lived to be one hundred, I had plenty of opportunities to observe and learn from other daughters. An army of us populated waiting rooms, malls, pharmacies, hair salons, libraries, rehab centers, hospital corridors, parks, hearing aid centers, coffee shops, bookstores, galleries, dentists' offices. Everywhere Alice and I went, daughters were helping their mothers, or in some cases fathers, to see, hear, communicate, and move from place to place. Look. You'll see them.

Sometimes I think about that sixty-something daughter in the checkout line. Now that I have more information and experience, I can speculate about her in a way I couldn't that day. Maybe she had gotten her bank statement and saw that another thousand dollars had dropped away. Maybe worry had distracted her from hearing her mother's joke about the movie stars. Maybe she'd never liked her mother and wasn't about to start now and had good reasons.

I'm sure my judgment was probably harsher than she deserved. Whatever her truth at that moment, I respect it. I'm also grateful I concluded what I did at the time because it helped me find my way. Despite challenges, Alice and I stuck together emotionally, psychically, and physically to the end. This is not to say we didn't hit bumps. Some derailed us for days and some were minor. Nevertheless, we found grace. We both worked at that, and also we were lucky. Alice made new friends, and I had the devoted support of my friends of many years, and caring readers of a blog I wrote regularly about my mother and me, *Go Ask Alice . . . When She's 94.*

Recently, I came across a mother/daughter pair in a parking garage. They were giggling about something when the elevator doors swept open and I saw them inside. Both wore white polo shirts, pressed slacks, and pixie haircuts. I got on and when the elevator started to ascend again, the daughter's hand quickly reached out to steady her mother, who used a cane. I knew she did this automatically and often because her purpose during this phase of her life is to accompany, advocate for, and watch over her mother, the woman who had done these things for her a long time ago.

I stood apart from them. Their shared laughter was their own. I thought about Alice and how it's not reasonable to want your mother to live more than a century. Still, sometimes when I hear a mother and daughter laughing, I wish could be leaning over to catch some funny remark in a waiting room or bringing flowers to her, a gesture that would always, always thrill her.

The elevator dinged. The pixie-cut mother and daughter slowly walked toward their car, and I began to cry as I walked toward mine. I felt, as I had for a long time after Alice died, like a branch broken off a tree.

I've left being a caregiver behind, but there are still days when I need to push myself to carve purpose from the stubborn stone of a so-called "carefree" life. Even without Alice, I still look for those mother/daughter pairings. When one comes into view, I usually try to make eye contact with the daughter and, if I can do that, I nod at her: *I see you, and I know what you do.*

Between Worlds

I looked up from my laptop to let my eyes rest on the flow of the river and spotted several vultures circling the dike across from my houseboat. Morning. Already hot outside. Black bodied and red faced as if embarrassed by their occupation, turkey vultures barely flap their wings as they circle, but two of them grew tired of even that little bit of effort. They descended to rest on a pair of posts bearing a No Trespassing sign, a good enough parking area until whatever was dying on the riverbank finished the hard work that task can sometimes be.

Living in the country across from a sparsely populated island, as I have lived for over forty years, I'm no stranger to either the beauty or the relentless business of nature. I wasn't surprised when several more of these large and graceful birds glided down to the grass a few moments later. The two trespassers then lifted off, flew low a hundred yards or so, and disappeared into some weeds.

I'd already been thinking about death that morning. I'd been in contact with a friend whose dog was sick, and our conversation made me think about the deaths of my dogs, the pain of those losses. I felt a rush of gratitude again for their companionship, staggered as they were several years apart in what's turning out to be a long life.

I lowered my head, tapped the track pad. When the screen on my laptop lit up again, I returned to the writing task at hand. With a pile of work waiting to be done, I decided not to indulge in vultures and grief.

An hour or so later, as I was eating lunch, a great white egret came down from the clear blue sky to stretch its legs along the opposite bank, quite a distance from the vultures. Feast over, only a few of them still remained to pick bones. They didn't seem to notice the newcomer.

I'd never seen an egret so near to the moorage. They usually stay inland a bit, around the lake on the island. I observed its careful stalk and concentration and took some photos to commemorate the occasion. I chalked it up to good manners when the large bird turned away from me to gulp down a fish. I felt glad not to watch, but I thought, *Death again*. Later, when I looked at the photos I'd taken, they were only blurs of something white.

After a couple more hours at the computer, I decided to climb the ramp and go for a walk before dinner. I soon found myself in the woods thinking about, and deeply missing, my dogs again and all of our walks through those same woods. The exchange with my friend seemed to have called all three back to my heart.

I pictured each of them in my mind and thought about how fast they all were—either whippet or greyhound mixes, all of them tan and white and swift as a deer. Just as I thought *swift as a deer*, I happened to turn and peer through some leaves. A little doe stood not far away, looking at me, and she was wearing a collar.

She didn't move. I didn't move. I've seen deer before, of course, many times. But I squinted, hardly believing my eyes at the sight of that collar. I stared, expecting it to fall off. I told myself, it's not a collar. How could it be a collar? It must be a bit of debris that she's picked up when passing through some bushes.

She turned her head slightly and stepped forward into a small clearing where I could see her a bit better. The collar, dark brown, stayed in place. It appeared to be a sort of chain but made of something natural, not a metal chain—nothing governmental or official from the Department of Fish and Wildlife. It draped over her neck, resting against her tan chest. She glanced at me again before walking slowly off into the trees and out of sight. Before she left, I tried to take a photo, but again, as with the egret, my phone camera captured mostly a blur.

That night before bed, I lit three candles, one for each dog. I breathed deeply for a while, closed my eyes, then summoned each of them by name—Carson, Boon, Brio. They came in twilight, that crack between worlds. This was the light given, not conjured. We were on the northern Oregon coast, another place of many walks and runs together. They seemed overjoyed as they ran to me. I wept as I greeted them.

What does the whole of it mean—the vultures, the misplaced tall white bird, the deer wearing a collar, a visit from my three, long-gone best friends? Will I die soon? Will all of these creatures and others from my life, maybe even a few humans, meet me in the twilight when I do? Or does it all add up to no such thing, nothing at all?

Once, I would have chased these thoughts around. I would have tried to sharpen up the photographs and puzzled over the meaning. But now I am old. Some of these days are not like the others. I don't need to fathom everything each one brings. I only need to live them, as they come. To be an old woman is a marvelous thing.

ACKNOWLEDGMENTS

No writer could ask for a smarter, wiser, or more gifted partner in the making of a book than my literary agent, Kerry D'Agostino, at Curtis Brown, Ltd. Our bond has validated my belief in the creative and empathic power of intergenerational relationships. I feel lucky beyond belief to get to work with her.

Kerry D'Agostino connected me with OSU Press. My thanks to everyone who is part of this legendary Oregon publisher, and especially to Kim Hogeland for taking a chance on *There Was an Old Woman* and standing behind it all the way, as well as for giving excellent guidance throughout the writing; to Micki Reaman for her close, thoughtful reading and extraordinary editorial eye; and to Marty Brown for her gift of somehow making it fun to talk about spreading the word. Writers Bette Husted and Evelyn Hess were contacted by OSU Press to give early and careful readings of the manuscript, and I'm beholden to them for their astute remarks and support.

I'm indebted to my friend, Joanne Mulcahy, for her sustained encouragement, wisdom, and suggestions. From the first essay to the last, Joanne's contributions have been invaluable. Her questions along the way opened worlds of thought. These pages wouldn't exist as a book without her.

I'm grateful to Meg Glaser for her loving support, patience (bottomless wells of patience), and generosity throughout the years it took to complete this project. I thank her for her unwavering faith in it and in me and for always urging me in the direction of balance with regard to many of the subjects brought up in these pieces.

Heartfelt thanks to early and late readers of this work: Julia Helfritz, Thalia Zepatos, Ruth Gundle, and Justin Ting, and to Esther Podemski for her considered reading of early drafts of "The Old Woman in Time."

To the friends who provided an always gentle but firm wind at my back as I wrote, your presence means the world to me: Salli Archibald, Katharine and Alan Cahn, Leigh Coffey, Bob Hazen, Claudia Johnson, Teresa Jordan, Ketzel Levine, Michael and Petra Mathers, Scott Lyons, Diane Mcdevitt, Kathy Moriarty, Sandra Sedgwick, Judy Teufel, and Susan Walsh. Daily walks and talks with Julia Helfritz kept me going through many ups, downs, zigzags, and roundabouts with this project.

Special thanks to Theo Le Guin, who made it possible to use the poems of Ursula K. Le Guin in these pages.

Several older women in my life shined a light on the path, but most especially Alice, Mattie, Eleanor, and Ursula. I am humbled by their patience with my limitations in understanding when they lived the years I'm living now and truly thankful for all the love. I hold my memories of each of them close.

SELECTED READING

(Fiction that centers, or includes an emphasis on, older characters)

An Unnecessary Woman, Rabih Alameddine

The Twilight Years, Sawako Ariyoshi

The Woman from Tantoura, Radwa Ashour, translated by Kay Heikkinen

The Elegance of the Hedgehog, Muriel Barbery

The Lady in the Van, Alan Bennett

Unexpected Lessons in Love, Bernadine Bishop

Three Things About Elsie, Joanna Cannon

The Hearing Trumpet, Leonora Carrington

Fellowship Point, Alice Elliot Dark

Fire on the Mountain, Anita Desai

The Dark Flood Rises, Margaret Drabble

The Witch of Exmoor, Margaret Drabble

All the News I Need, Joan Frank

The Autobiography of Miss Jane Pittman, Ernest J. Gaines

Frangipani House, Beryl Gilroy

Women on the Run, Janet Campbell Hale

Our Souls at Night, Kent Haruf

Elizabeth is Missing, Emma Healey

The Buried Giant, Kazuo Ishiguro

The Old Woman and the River, Ismail Fahad Ismail, translated by Sophia Vasalou

Live a Little, Howard Jacobsen

The Summer Book, Tove Jansson

Time After Time, Molly Keane

The Stone Angel, Margaret Laurence

The Diary of a Good Neighbor, Jane Somers (Doris Lessing)

How It All Began, Penelope Lively

Like a Mule Bringing Ice Cream to the Sun, Sarah Ladipo Manyika

These Foolish Things, Deborah Moggach

The Little House, Kyoko Nakajima,
    translated by Ginny Tapley Takemori

Mama Day, Gloria Naylor

Purge, Sofi Oksanen, translated by Lola Rogers

The Woman Next Door, Yewande Omotoso

Emily, Alone, Stewart O'Nan

Elena Knows, Claudia Piñeiro, translated by Frances Riddle

Quartet in Autumn, Barbara Pym

Some Tame Gazelle, Barbara Pym

Still Life with Breadcrumbs, Anna Quindlen

Lillian Boxfish Takes a Walk, Kathleen Rooney

All Passion Spent, Vita Sackville-West

A Reckoning, May Sarton

As We Are Now, May Sarton

The Education of Harriet Hatfield, May Sarton

The Dictionary of Animal Languages, Heidi Sopinka

Memento Mori, Muriel Spark

Olive Kitteridge, Elizabeth Strout

Olive, Again, Elizabeth Strout

The Door, Magda Szabo, translated by Len Rix

Mrs. Palfrey at the Claremont, Elizabeth Taylor

Drive Your Plow Over the Bones of the Dead, Olga Tokarczuk,
    translated by Antonia Lloyd-Jones

A Spool of Blue Thread, Anne Tyler

Clock Dance, Anne Tyler

Unquiet, Linn Ullman

The Enchanted April, Elizabeth von Armin

Two Old Women, Velma Wallis

Rhode Island Blues, Fay Weldon

Jumping the Queue, Mary Wesley

Meet Me at the Museum, Anne Youngson